Hidcote

The Garden and
Lawrence Johnston

HIDCOTE

The Garden and
Lawrence Johnston
Graham S Pearson

THE NATIONAL TRUST

To Susan

for her encouragement,

support and assistance

First published in the United Kingdom in 2007 by
National Trust Books
151 Freston Road
London
W10 6TH

An imprint of Anova Books Company Ltd.

Text for *History of the Garden* © Graham S Pearson
Text for *Tour of the Garden* © Anna Pavord
Design and layout copyright © 2007 National Trust Books
Designed by Bet Ayer and Lee-May Lim

ISBN 9781905400539

A CIP record for this book is available from the British Library.

Printed and bound by SNP Leefung Printers Limited, China
Colour reproduction by Spectrum Colour Ltd., England

10 9 8 7 6 5 4 3 2 1

This book can be ordered direct from the publisher.
Please contact the marketing department.
But try your bookshop first.

Page 1: Seat in the Lime Arbour.
Page 2: The Red Borders looking towards the Gazebos
and the Stilt Garden with Heaven's Gate beyond.
Page 4: The Beech Avenue looking north towards the gates
copied from those at Cleeve Prior in Jekyll and Weaver's
Gardens for Small Country Houses.

Contents

Acknowledgements

I am especially grateful to Mike Beeston and Glyn Jones, Property Manager and Head Gardener respectively, and all the team at Hidcote for their encouragement and assistance in the writing of this book. I would also like to thank the many individuals in both Britain and abroad who have provided information and assisted my search for information about Lawrence Johnston and Hidcote: John Balmford, Gwen Bell, Marguerite Bell, Audrey Bowker, Ewen Buchanan, Derek C. Bull, Ned Carter, Margaret Fisher, Henri Garrigue, Jane Glennie, Alan Hall, Ann Hettich, Christine Hiskey, Bernard Jeanty, M K Miles, Gerard Noel, Edwin Nutbourne, Rosemary Powell, Maurice Ribbans, Ros Roberts, Jack Sully, Gordon Thompson, James M Waterbury, Doris Williams, and Edward Wilson.

Many thanks go also to Melanie Aspey, director of the Rothschild Institute; Denis Edelin of the United States National Archives and Record Administration (NARA) in Washington, DC; Brett Elliott, Archivist and Librarian of the Royal Horticultural Society; Mary Hodgson of the Legal Section of the National Trust; Elliott O'Neill of the Maryland Historical Society; Leonie Paterson of the Royal Botanic Garden Edinburgh; Sindy Pagan of the Woodlawn Cemetery, New York; Iain Shaw and Dan Williams of the Records Section of the National Trust; Jonathan Smith of Trinity College, Cambridge, and Roberta Twinn of 'A Soldier's Life', Discovery Museum, Newcastle-upon-Tyne. I would also like to thank the Archives de Paris, the Chipping Campden Library, the Campden and District Historical Association (CADHAS), the Evesham Library, the Mairies of Ferney, Menton and Nice, Her Majesty's Court Service, the National Archives, the Oxford County Studies Library, the Seattle Public Library, and the United States National Archives and Record Administration (NARA) in both Morrow, Georgia and Seattle, Washington.

Looking across the Old Garden towards the Manor House with the Cedar of Lebanon on the right.

Introduction

Lawrence Johnston and his mother.

In 1907 Mrs Gertrude Winthrop bought Hidcote, some 116 hectares (287 acres) on one of the northern outliers of the Cotswolds between Chipping Campden and Stratford-upon-Avon. In doing so she provided her son, Lawrence Johnston, with the opportunity to create one of the most beautiful gardens in England. This he did, establishing the major planting over a period of some 20 years, drawing chiefly upon the principles and ideas set out by Thomas Mawson in *The Arts and Crafts of Garden Making*, in addition to exchanging ideas and plants with noted garden experts of the day.

As a keen gardener from a wealthy family, Johnston was able to introduce many new and attractive plants to Hidcote and, from the 1920s, became involved in plant-hunting expeditions – either personally, or through funding them as a member of syndicates of similarly wealthy garden enthusiasts. By this means, the garden was enriched by exotic and unusual plants from locations as diverse as the Alps, the Andes, South Africa, Mount Kilimanjaro, Formosa (Taiwan) and Yunnan, in southwestern China.

During its heyday in the 1930s and 1940s Hidcote opened to the public for a few days each year at an entrance fee of a shilling per visitor, with the proceeds going to charity. Following World War II, Lawrence Johnston, then in his mid-seventies, offered Hidcote to the National Trust and, in August 1948, it became the first garden accepted under a Gardens Fund set up jointly by the Royal Horticultural Society and the National Trust. Johnston was assured that he would be welcome to return to live at Hidcote and be in charge of the garden and that, when he was in residence, the garden would not open to the public for more than three days a week. But in the end he came back only once, for two months in the summer of 1950, and lived the remainder of his life at his other garden on the French Riviera, Serre de la Madone. He died there on 27 April 1958 and is buried alongside his mother in Mickleton churchyard, a mile from Hidcote.

In the early years funding for Hidcote was always a problem for the National Trust, since the garden had been accepted without an endowment. But in recent years a combination of significant donations and an increase in visitor numbers has made Hidcote self-financing, and the future for this glorious garden is now bright. Today, some 130,000 visitors annually enjoy a garden that differs little from that first described in two articles from 1930, in *Country Life*, and further articles dating from the height of the garden's development, in the 1940s. Hidcote remains a leading example of a garden in Arts and Crafts style and is, quite justifiably, one of the most popular gardens in England.

Painting of flowers by Lawrence Johnston, which was originally a mural at Kiftsgate and today is seen in the Manor House by visitors on their way to the garden. The painting includes cardoon, iris, lilies, lupins, poppies, primulas and violas.

1. Lawrence Johnston's Early Years

Hidcote's founder, Lawrence Waterbury Johnston, was born in Paris on 12 October 1871, first son of an affluent, well-connected American family. His parents, Elliott, from a wealthy banking family, and Gertrude (née Waterbury), were each related to the First Lady of a United States President, albeit almost a century apart.

Johnston's father served in the United States Navy from an early age, subsequently resigning to join the Confederate forces in the American Civil War, in 1861, where he served in General 'Stonewall' Jackson's brigade, and lost a leg in the battle of Antietam, a year later. Johnston's uncle, Henry Elliott Johnston, married Harriet Lane, First Lady to President James Buchanan.

His mother came from a wealthy New York family who had made their money from rope making, and were distantly related to Eleanor Roosevelt. Lawrence himself was the first of three children all born in France, although the youngest, Elisabeth, died of whooping cough in infancy. Johnston's father regularly travelled to the United States, but it was not until 1875 that the whole family travelled from France to New York. By the mid-1880s Johnston's parents had divorced, and his father remarried shortly afterwards. His mother, with Lawrence and his younger brother, Elliott, spent much of the next few years in Europe, subsequently in London marrying Charles Francis ('Frank') Winthrop, a retired Wall Street businessman who lived mostly in Paris, and did not participate significantly in Gertrude's active social life. Gertrude Winthrop, as she was now, enjoyed the high society of the 1890s, occasionally in the company of her sons or husband, and moved between engagements in New York, New Jersey and Maine on a regular basis. Lawrence Johnston spent the years 1893–97 in England, initially in preparation for entrance to Trinity College, Cambridge, at a privately run establishment in nearby Little Shelford, and then at Trinity College itself. He graduated in 1897, with a Bachelor of Arts degree.

Returning to Little Shelford for a year after his graduation, Johnston then spent some time as a farming pupil at The Grange, New Etal, Cornhill-on-Tweed, where he lodged with a gentleman farmer, George Laing, and his wife Annie. Perhaps the seeds of Johnston's interest in planting and gardening, which were to come to such marvellous fruition in future years, were sown around this time, although at this stage his interest was mainly in agriculture.

In 1900 Johnston successfully applied for naturalization as a British subject. His formal petition, completed and sworn in front of a Justice of the Peace on 10 January, declared that he wished to become a British citizen from a 'desire to serve in the Imperial Yeomanry about to be sent to South Africa.'

Indeed his military record, dating from 11 January 1900, the day after he had made his declaration in London for naturalization, shows that he joined the Imperial Yeomanry as Private 3,296 in the 15th (Northumberland and Durham) Company. He sailed for South Africa in February, was promoted to Second Lieutenant on 12 October 1901 and then, only a week later, to Lieutenant. On his return from South Africa on the *Braemar Castle*, in 1902, he was appointed Second Lieutenant in the Northumberland Hussars Yeomanry and, a month later, appointed an Honorary Lieutenant in the Army. Subsequently, he was promoted to Captain in May 1909 and Major in June 1913. He continued to serve in the Northumberland Hussars, a territorial force with annual summer camps, until reaching the age limit in 1922. His record shows that he was 5 feet 8 inches tall, had fluent conversational French and was a Roman Catholic. We also know that he had blue eyes and fair brown hair.

Johnston probably returned to live in Northumberland, at New Etal, but then a year or so later moved back to Little Shelford. Evidently his enthusiasm for horticulture was by now

THE NATURALIZATION ACT, 1870.

LIST of ALIENS to whom Certificates of Naturalization or of Readmission to British Nationality have been granted by the Secretary of State under the provisions of the Act 33 Vic., cap. 14, and have been registered in the Home Office pursuant to the Act during the Month of January, 1900.

Name.	Country.	Date of Certificate.	Place of Residence.
Johnston, Lawrence ...	United States of America	25th January, 1900 ...	Northumberland, New Etal, Cornhill-on-Tweed

Extract from *The London Gazette*, 2 February 1900 showing the Certificate of Naturalization for Lawrence Johnston issued on 25 January 1900.

well established, since the *Journal of the Royal Horticultural Society* records him as one of the 40 Fellows elected to membership at the General Meeting of 5 April 1904. His keen interest in gardening is apparent in records from the RHS Lindley Library, from 1905, which show the first of numerous book loans (see below).

Books borrowed by Lawrence Johnston from the RHS Library between April and November 1905:

Alpine Plants, W A Clark
Les Plantes des Alpes, H Correvon
Alpine Flora, Hoffmann
Alpine Flowers for Gardens, Robinson
Atlas de la Flora Alpines (5 tomes & Index)
Plant Breeding, L H Bailey
Book of the Wild Garden, S Fitzherbert
Book of Climbing Plants, S Arnott
The Book of Bulbs, S Arnott
History of Gardening in England, Amherst
Garden Craft, T H Mawson
Century Book of Gardening, E T Cook

Meanwhile his mother maintained her socialite lifestyle, spending some time in Berlin before returning to New York and the East Coast. Johnston, with valet in tow, sailed from Liverpool to join her for a period in 1906, before her departure for a summer in Europe and his return to England to fulfil a military obligation. A contemporary court circular, from 10 July 1906, records a royal visit by King Edward VII to Alnwick Castle, Northumberland. A royal procession marked the opening of a new rail bridge over the Tyne, escorted by the Northumberland Hussars, under the command of one Lieutenant L Johnston.

While neither Johnston's military engagements nor his mother's packed social calendar give any indication of their imminent interest in Hidcote, further records of Johnston's borrowing from the RHS Lindley Library show that he may have had garden planning on his mind. Titles he borrowed in 1907, only five months before coming to Hidcote, included *Home and Garden* and *Wood and Garden*, both by Gertrude Jekyll, and Algernon-Freeman Mitford's *The Bamboo Garden*.

2. Arriving at Hidcote in 1907

The Hidcote Manor estate, which includes the village of Hidcote Bartrim with its dozen or so cottages, occupies a largely level plateau, sheltered from the east winds some 183 metres (600 feet) above sea level in the northern outliers of the Cotswolds. It lies on the Gloucester-Warwickshire border, about 1.6 km (1 mile) east of Mickleton, 6.5 km (4 miles) north of Chipping Campden and 16 km (10 miles) south of Stratford-upon-Avon.

The manor house, built in the 17th century as a farm house, passed through several hands before it was inherited from the Freeman family, early in 1907, by John Tucker, who had been farming there since 1873. Within a couple of months of probate being granted the estate was put up for auction and advertised in *The Times* on 22 June 1907 as 'a valuable freehold farm comprising some 287 acres and 34 perches to be sold by auction at the Noel Arms in Chipping Campden on Tuesday 2 July 1907 with possession on 29 September 1907' – Michaelmas Day (29 September) was the date on which most agricultural leases began and ended. The advertisement stated that the land would be sold together with the 'very substantial and picturesque farm house, stone built, with entrance hall, fine oak staircase, three sitting rooms, eight bed rooms, two box rooms, and usual offices, with lawns and large kitchen garden' and went on to note that 'the farm is particularly healthy, being situated on a spur of the Cotswolds at an elevation of from 500 to 800 feet above sea level and from it extensive views of the counties of Warwick, Worcester and Gloucester can be obtained. Meets of the Warwickshire, North Cotswold and Haythrop [sic] Hounds are within easy distance, and the partridge shooting on the estate is good.'

Hidcote lies behind the clump of trees on the skyline just to the right of the tower of Chipping Campden Church.

Plan, Particulars, and Conditions of Sale

OF AN ESTATE AT

HIDCOTE BARTRIM,

GLOUCESTERSHIRE,

Three Miles from Campden and Long Marston Stations and Five Miles from Honeybourne Station, G.W.R.

VALUABLE AND DESIRABLE

FREEHOLD ESTATE.

HUTCHINGS AND DEER

Are favoured with instructions from the Owner to Sell by Auction, at the

Noel Arms Hotel, Chipping Campden,

On TUESDAY, the 2nd day of JULY, 1907,

At Five o'clock in the Afternoon, subject to the conditions of Sale annexed,

ALL THAT VALUABLE

FREEHOLD FARM,

COMPRISING

287a. 0r. 34p.

In 48 Enclosures, of which 134a. 3r. 19p. is Pasture, 141a. 0r. 26p. Arable, and 11a. 0r. 28p. Coppices, Woodland, Houses, and Buildings, together with the

VERY SUBSTANTIAL AND PICTURESQUE FARM HOUSE,

With Lawns and large Kitchen Garden,

Convenient and Substantial Farm Buildings,

AND

TEN COTTAGES

All of which is and has for 34 years past been in the occupation of Mr. John Tucker.

The Farm is in a good state of cultivation and will be sold with possession at Michaelmas next. Part of the Arable is good light land, the remainder being a rich loam with enough staple to grow corn of any description, or roots which can be eaten on.

The Pasture is excellent, and adapted for Dairying and Stock Rearing, and some of the enclosures will feed.

The Home and Farm are particularly healthy, being from 600 to 800 feet above sea level, and are approached and intersected by good roads.

There is an excellent bed of stone on the Property, with a Quarry which has been worked very remuneratively.

There are about 3 acres of good and productive Orcharding.

The House and Buildings are nearly all stone, with slated or tiled roofs in good condition.

The Property is well watered, the supply to the House and Buildings being laid on from the Hill.

Sales particulars for the auction of the Hidcote Manor estate.

THE RESIDENCE

Is a very picturesque and substantial stone erection with a tiled roof, has a good elevation, and comprises Entrance Hall, with fine Oak Staircase, two Sitting Rooms, Office, Kitchen and Larder, 4 Bedrooms and 2 Dressing Rooms on the first floor, with 4 good Attics or Bedrooms and Box-room over. Large paved Court, Back Kitchen and Dairy with Granary over (Stone with Slated Roof), Washhouse, Coalhouse, and 2 w.c.'s.

There are Lawns in front and on the south side of the House, with fine shrubs and a nice Summer House, and a large and productive Kitchen Garden. Adjoining is a Tennis Lawn and small Nut Orchard.

Near the Court is the Nag Stable for 4 Horses with a good room over, and saddle room adjoining.

A plentiful supply of good water is laid on from the Hills to the House, Garden, and Buildings.

More especially relevant, given the subsequent development of the garden, the sales particulars described the residence as being 'very picturesque', with the garden comprising 'lawns in front and on the south side of the House, with fine shrubs and a nice Summer House, and a large and productive Kitchen Garden.'

At the July 1907 auction, the Hidcote estate had reached £6,500 by the point at which it was withdrawn from sale. Three weeks later, Johnston, acting on behalf of his mother, contracted with John Tucker to purchase the estate for £7,200, and paid a deposit of £10. Johnston was appointed agent because his redoubtable mother was about to sail from Southampton for the bright lights of New York, arriving there on 7 August. The actual conveyance of the estate took place on 30 September 1907, in a deed signed by the said Mrs Winthrop, with a mortgage of £4,000 that was subsequently discharged in November 1913. Johnston and his mother arrived at Hidcote in October 1907 – although, naturally, she was soon to depart again for New York.

The next few years saw work being carried out on both the garden and the house, the latter being linked to a neighbouring building to provide further accommodation. A plan of 1913 (see opposite) shows the original building's ground floor as having a dining room, drawing room, sitting room and hall, with the dining room linked by a passageway leading to the adjoining building containing the kitchen, larder, housekeeper's room, servant's hall, scullery, dairy and laundry.

By this time the upper floors of both buildings were bedrooms and the plan also shows that central heating had been fitted.

Hidcote's famous garden very nearly failed to develop past the initial stages since, after only five years, Johnston's mother considered selling up and moving to somewhere near Bath. Although possibly related in some way to the sudden death of Johnston's younger brother, Elliot, at the age of 40 in early 1912, it was more likely that Mrs Winthrop was seeking softer water. A letter of December 1912, from her solicitor to Messrs Bruton, Knowles & Co., Estate Agents of Gloucester, states that a well-to-do American lady, a Mrs Winthrop of Hidcote, was looking for a thoroughly reliable firm in connection with the contemplated sale of Hidcote. It goes on to explain that Mrs Winthrop was a widow, with a grown-up son by her first husband, adding perhaps somewhat ominously that she was 'restless and fidgety, and likes to have her own way, but is otherwise quite a nice old lady & very active' and

Details about the residence contained in the sales particulars.

that 'rightly or wrongly she considers she has been taken advantage of in the past in connection with the management of her property, & hence her desire for someone she can thoroughly trust & who will be quite frank with her.' In summary, the letter remarks that the lady in question had spent a great deal of money on Hidcote and that 'her idea of leaving is due to reasons of health which she attributes to the hardness of the water, soft water almost being a mania with her.' A subsequent letter says that the climate does not suit her and asks Bruton, Knowles & Co. to place the property on their books, adding that 'the property, together with the extensive additions and alterations which have been made, has cost our client about £16,000.'

There follows a delay until May 1913 because (as perhaps one might have guessed) Mrs Winthrop was going to be away and did not wish the estate agents to visit until she had returned and the alterations currently in progress at Hidcote were completed. Her letter to the agents suggests that the matter is now somewhat less pressing, remarking that 'I do think it would be wiser for us to look for some other place first, before giving up Hidcote, & I may write to you about it & ask if you know of anything which might suit us', and by May her solicitor writes again to say that 'she appears to have made up her mind to dispose of the Hidcote property, but is in no particular hurry, and is at present looking round to see what else she can find to suit her', with an imminent visit to inspect a property near Bath mentioned, since 'the great essentials are soft water and mild climate.' The matter then lapses as, unsurprisingly, Mrs Winthrop is again away. In December 1913 a possible purchaser for Hidcote offering £15,000 is mentioned, although the estate agent is now checking the situation 'as Mrs Winthrop may have changed her mind about selling'. The reply from her solicitor confirms that 'we doubt however whether she is now likely to desire to sell.' In January 1914 an obviously frustrated estate agent informs her representative that the prospective purchaser will not view unless Mrs Winthrop has definitely made up her mind to sell, adding that the asking price is a high one. But later that year saw the start of World War I, putting an end to any further shenanigans, and so ensuring Hidcote's future as the site of Johnston's world-famous garden.

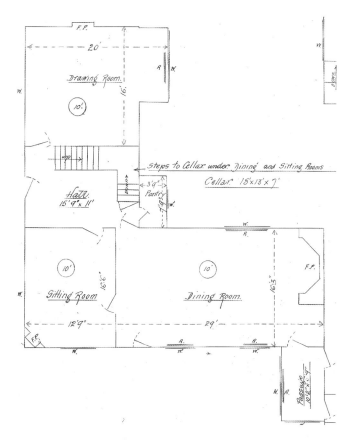

Ground floor plan of the Manor House in 1913.

3. Creating the Garden

The first published account of the garden, a 1930 *Country Life* article by Avray Tipping, described the garden prior to Lawrence Johnston's arrival as having on the south side a sloping lawn with a cedar tree and some flower beds forming a small pleasure garden, enclosed from the utilitarian sections and the fields. The general slope was southward, while westward was a modest but immediate rise, eastward a slight dip before a sharp ascent, and in the northward direction more or less level ground. Since Hidcote was surrounded by arable fields and pastures to the south, west and north, there was little shelter from prevailing winds.

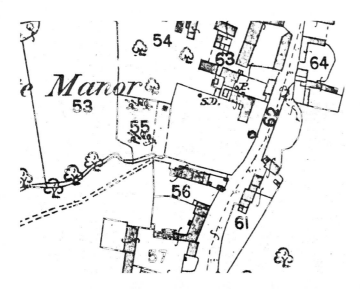

The Ordnance Survey map of 1885 (above) shows the area around the house was composed of a grass bank (54), a house ground (53), a paddock and buildings (55), the house and garden (63), a nut orchard (56), buildings and yard (57) with cottages and gardens (61) across the village road, which is described as a road and lawn (62).

Thomas Mawson's *The Art and Craft of Garden Making* was one of the many books that Johnston had borrowed from the Royal Horticultural Society Library during his time at Little Shelford, and the author's principles evidently became Johnston's guiding light in developing Hidcote. Mawson's book describes the styles of laying out gardens, identifying what is commendable in each. Successive chapters deal first with the selection of a site and then how lawns should be laid out, terrace and flower gardens created, hedges and fences, summer houses, water gardens and ponds constructed, as well as conservatories and kitchen gardens; there is little doubt that Johnston was very conscious of Mawson's advice, since there are so many echoes in Hidcote's design. Mawson in particular recommends formality 'near the house, merging into the natural by degrees, so as to attach the house by imperceptible gradations to the general landscape', and this is exactly how Lawrence Johnston developed Hidcote, where the 'garden rooms' and enclosed areas, provide such an astonishing variety of topiary, plantings, paving, water features and unexpected vistas. They certainly reflect Mawson's belief that:

> the arrangement should suggest a series of apartments rather than a panorama which can be grasped in one view: art is well directed in arousing curiosity, always inviting further exploration, to be rewarded with new but never a final discovery.

Johnston started work on Hidcote's garden soon after taking possession of the land. The 1901 census record and annual electoral registers provide a means of deducing the names of the workers he employed. Living at Hidcote Bartrim at that time were Alfred Hughes, Thomas Newman, and William Pearce as were Ernest Daniels and Tom Handy: Edward Pearce and his brother (presumably Jim Pearce), both sons of William Pearce, worked on the garden, as did members of the Hughes family, while Ernest Daniels was the chauffeur.

The development of Hidcote proceeded apace, with Johnston leaving, almost literally, no stone unturned. In fact the large Cedar of Lebanon to the south and the walls to the Old Garden are all that remain of Hidcote before his arrival. The original main entrance to the house was from the east, with steps up from the village road to a lawn, flanked by specimens of variegated holly and cypress. The lawn was separated from the road by an ornate iron fence above a stone retaining wall, with further stone steps leading to a short path to the front door. Johnston changed the main entrance to the house so that it was now on the north side, approached from the courtyard. On the east side he created a cobbled parterre garden, raising the wall between the garden and the village road and decorating it with urns.

In developing the Old Garden with its two apartments, or garden rooms, below the Cedar Lawn, Johnston was evidently following Mawson's principle that: 'working outwards from the house, dispose the terraces as the falls of the land allow, and the height of the house demands, according as the original disposition of the land suggests.'

Mawson goes on to say that, in designing a garden, 'attention would first be directed to discovering and framing those features visible from it which have in them the elements of the picturesque, or which in any way give character and individuality to the site' and notes that nothing is prettier than a vista through the 'smooth-shaven green alley' or an archway framing a view of the countryside beyond:

> … it is for the creation of such effects that the designer must aim in the arrangements of his terraces and particularly their steps and the placing of seats, arbours and bastions so as to emphasise them when created, at the same time taking care that the balance and symmetry of the scheme as a whole are not endangered in the treatment of individual features.

Furthermore he avows that 'gates may advantageously mark the end of a vista' – a suggestion that Johnston used to good effect at Hidcote, at several points at the ends of the long axes of the garden: from the Cedar Lawn to Heaven's Gate, from the Gazebos to the gates at the end of the Long Walk, and again with the Beech Avenue.

Lawrence Johnston with his dogs and gardeners.

Mrs Winthrop with staff.

Left: Hidcote Manor House in 1907 with the entrance up steps from the village road.

Left: The same view (as above) today, showing the wall and ornamental urns that Johnston had made when he changed the courtyard entrance into the main entrance to the house.

In about 1910 the Cedar Lawn had no hedging and lacked steps down to the lawn between the herbaceous beds in the Old Garden, although some trellis work to the south shows that the land sloped gently in that direction.

Johnston put a semicircular seat by the cedar tree to provide emphasis at the eastern end of the vista as recommended by Thomas Mawson.

Above left: The view towards the Cedar Lawn and the house in 1907–8 before Johnston introduced the steps and planted a hedge around the Cedar Lawn.

Below right: The same view today showing the steps from the Cedar Lawn and in the distance the semicircular seat.

Below left: A semicircular seat illustrated in Thomas Mawson's *Art and Crafts of Garden Making*.

Below right: The semicircular seat under the Cedar of Lebanon reinstated in the winter of 2002.

Slightly later, he planted a hedge with topiary birds around the Cedar Lawn, to the west providing a gateway to the trees beyond. Today there are no topiary birds at this point but, instead, a well-developed box hedge.

The two small garden rooms, the Maple Garden and White Garden, south of the Cedar Lawn, are enclosed by yew hedges. Both gardens are just over 1 metre (3.5 feet) below the level of the Cedar Lawn and are reached by a few steps. The Maple Garden has changed little since its introduction but Johnston changed the White Garden's squat pillar under the sundial, surrounded by a grass circle and rose beds, for a slender pillar from the dismantled second Kew Bridge and added four small topiary birds.

Top: The Maple Garden shortly after Johnston created it during the first phase of the development of the garden in 1907–14.
Above: The same view today showing that little, apart from the seat, has changed.

Above right: The view from the Cedar Lawn through the Old Garden showing topiary birds and a vestigial hedge during the first phase of the garden's development 1907–14.
Right: The same view today showing the hedge around the Cedar Lawn.

History of the Garden

Today, the basic structure of the White Garden is largely unchanged apart from the grass circle having given way to paving and the sundial having been moved to Mrs Winthrop's Garden.

In the south border of the Old Garden, Johnston created one of several acid beds for rhododendrons, etc. A letter written by a 1920s visitor to Hidcote enthusiastically describes the preparation process in some detail:

1. Dig 3 foot deep, & lay 2 or 3 inches of clinkers (may be got from a railway station) on the ground. Cover these with a few inches of leaves or straw.
2. Fill in your bed with 3 parts leaf mould, decayed sawdust, & clinkers which have been broken up & then passed through an inch & a half sieve-mix the fine result of the clinkers with the other two parts.
3. The sawdust must be quite decayed look like mould. They found a sawmill where heaps of sawdust had been thrown out & left to all weathers for years – and this is what is decayed enough.
The plants growing in this compost are doing marvellously.

The beds were indeed filled with large amounts of sawdust (from Blockley sawmills) and clinker (from Campden station railway sidings), added to a lime-free loam and dug to a depth of 1 metre (3 feet). They were generally enclosed with slates, by which they can still be identified today.

Above: The White Garden in 1907–14 with a squat pillar under the sundial. Below right: The White Garden at a slightly later date with topiary birds and a slim pillar under the sundial that was later moved by Johnston to Mrs Winthrop's Garden. Below left: The White Garden today, with plump birds and the grass circle replaced by paving.

Further west, outside the Old Garden, a start was made on the Bathing Pool Garden with the provision of a small ground level pool. This is approached from the Circle by a few steps down into the Fuchsia Garden, some 0.6 metres (2 feet) lower, and then by some further steps to the Bathing Pool Garden, 1 metre (3 feet) below.

Topiary birds mark the top of the steps from the Fuchsia Garden whilst there are radiating beds from the other side of the pool. The farm buildings and cottages are visible through the trellis work in the background, as are the fields to the south west.

In about 1920, Johnston enlarged the pool, surrounding it by a low wall some 0.5 metres (18 inches) above the surrounding ground, increasing the depth to 0.64 metres (2 feet 1 inch) deep. In this he was following Mawson's suggestions almost to the letter:

> … where a fountain is well placed, it will form part of either a formal terrace scheme, or the central ornament in an old English formal garden such as a rose garden. … The best place for a fountain is an enclosed court of some kind … In such cases the light feathery streams may rise from the surface of the water, or where more elaboration is called for, a group of statuary, such as the boy and dolphin … may be introduced.

Below: The Bathing Pool Garden when first created in 1907–14 with its ground level pool and radiating beds in the foreground.
Below right: Bathing Pool Garden seen from the Fuchsia Garden with its topiary birds.

Right: Today, with its raised pool and boy and dolphin fountain similar to Thomas Mawson's recommendation in his influential book *The Art and Craft of Garden Making*.

Left: The Bathing
Pool Garden in the
1920s shows the
raised pool and the
thatched Italian
shelter.

Left: A similar view
of the Bathing Pool
Garden today.

It is interesting to note that during this period, Johnston was given an award of merit by the RHS at its show on 6 June 1911 for the Hidcote strain of *Primula pulverentula*. *The Times* article recorded that: 'Of the many new Chinese primroses none has spread from garden to garden so rapidly as *pulverentula*, but hitherto the typical crimson flowers only were known. The Hidcote strain adds the soft pinks from *Primula Japonica*, at the same time retaining the mealy stem and other characteristics of *pulverentula*.

The last features of the garden to be created during the first phase – between autumn 1907 and Johnston's departure in autumn 1914 to fight in World War I – were the Red Borders, running west towards where the Gazebos stand, and the Theatre Lawn to the north. Looking east towards the house there was trellis work around what is today the Circle. The topiary birds towards the Bathing Pool Garden are also visible. Trellis work runs along the southern edge of the Red Borders whilst to the north is a wall bordering the Theatre Lawn.

The tapestry hedging that surrounds the Circle is made up of holly mixed with copper beech, creating an effect associated with the Arts and Crafts style that Mawson described:

> In a pastoral landscape it is a source of delight to meet with mixed hedges of Holly, Thorn, Privet, Hornbeam and Beech, the various alternating hues and tints appealing strongly to those who are possessed of the painter's imaginative sense …

Johnston's active service in World War I, as a Major in the Northumberland Hussars, was initially short-lived. He received a shrapnel wound to the chest at Ypres in October 1914 and returned to England to become a patient at the King Edward VII's Hospital for Officers in London. The medical board considered his wound 'severe but not permanent' and estimated that he would be 'incapacitated for military duty for 10 weeks', a recuperative period during which Johnston read numerous books about gardening, plant houses and also plant hunting borrowed for him from the Royal Horticultural Society Library, some ten minutes' walk away. By May 1915 he was recovered, and back at Hidcote, but he returned to France in June 1916 and served until the end of the war, when he continued in what had become the Territorial Army until his retirement on reaching the age limit, on 31 October 1922. These interludes of military service meant that

The Theatre Lawn today shows that little has changed apart from the planting of replacement beeches on the raised area above the steps.

Johnston was only at Hidcote for a year during World War I and this, along with the fact that labour for the garden would have been scarce at this time, meant there was little major work on the garden until the next phase of development, beginning in 1918.

Even so, the Gazebos and the Stilt Garden to the west were both probably created during Johnston's recovery in 1915, before his return to France. Heaven's Gate beyond had also been built by this time, but without the later cherubs on top of the pillars, and there was as yet no hedge to the north along the Theatre Lawn. Today, both the Stilt Garden and the trees adjacent Heaven's Gate have developed further.

There must have been significant effort involved in creating the Stilt Garden as it is almost 1.2 metres (4 feet) above the height of the Red Borders, and a similar height above the path to the south that now runs alongside the Alpine Terrace.

The two Gazebos at Hidcote again reflect Mawson's advice that garden houses should serve to

… break up a somewhat flat expanse of garden and provide the antidote to a preponderance of horizontal lines, and at the same time supply convenient rest houses …the garden houses are placed equidistant from, and on either side of, the main axial line through the … grounds.

Below: The Red Borders and Gazebos in the mid-1910s showing the newly planted Stilt Garden beyond. Below right: The same view today showing the developed Stilt Garden with Heaven's Gate beyond.

In 1919 Johnston's mother purchased part of the neighbouring Hill Farm for £3,000. Since the land included an adjacent orchard to the south of Hidcote, this provided an opportunity to extend the garden further.

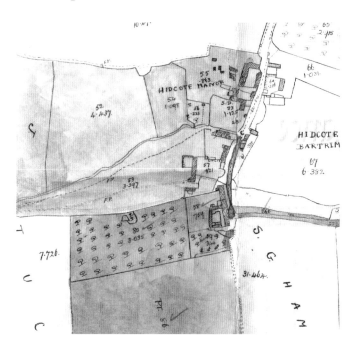

Above: The area coloured orange on the plan shows the part of Hill Farm to the south of Hidcote purchased in 1919, enabling the garden to be extended to the south.

The final phase of the development of the garden after World War I saw the laying out of the second main axis of the garden, running south from the Gazebos at right angles to the axis from the Cedar Lawn to the Stilt Garden. This formed the Long Walk, with further garden room apartments, Mrs Winthrop's Garden lying to the east and, to the west, the Pillar Garden. The Long Walk was constructed in two phases: the first, early in the 1920s, ending at the stream and the second, in the later 1920s, extending it further, to the gates at the end.

With regard to lawns, Johnston also took Mawson's advice on these 'distinctive features of English gardens' to heart:

> … by open stretches of grass, a restful effect is obtained, relieving the eye of too much detail, emphasizing the beauty of form and colour in trees, shrubs and flowers, and forming green glades to carry the eye forward into mellow distances.

Above: A 1930 *Country Life* view from the south Gazebo shows that the Long Walk had only recently been completed, and the hornbeam hedges on the far side of the stream have been newly planted.

Above: The Long Walk in the 1930s. The removable covers over the Alpine Terrace can be seen to the left of the Gazebo.

Left: Another 1930 *Country Life* photograph showing the view looking back through the gates along the Long Walk to the Gazebos.

The Pillar Garden with its yew pillars lying to the west of the Long Walk.

Mrs Winthrop's Garden lying to the east of the Long Walk showing the sundial on the slim pillar, originally in the White Garden, and beyond the beech hedge separating this garden from the Winter Border.

The Stream Garden, which runs across the Long Walk, is a type of garden whose charm, as Mawson notes, lies in the 'appearance of luxuriant, rampant, and almost tropical growth'. To the west of the Pillar Garden lies the Rock Bank, where Johnston, from the Stream Garden to the top of the Rock Bank simulated the rocky terrain from the Mediterranean to the Alpes-Maritimes, following Mawson's advice that rock gardens 'ought to have, above all things else, a definite plan, and should aim to reproduce some particular phase of nature'. He also followed his recommendation that it be 'secluded from the purely ornamental and formal parts of the grounds by a screen of pines and dark foliaged evergreens.'

Several plant shelters were built in the 1920s. One, over the Alpine Terrace, running south of and parallel to the Stilt Garden, had removable roof panels to provide protection to the alpines during the wet winter months. By the Lily Pool a larger plant shelter, approximately 17 by 5 metres (56 by 16 feet), housed a large collection of tender plants.

Below: An early photograph of the Rock Bank shows various alpine plants on a rock scree surface.

Right: The Rock Bank has been recently renovated with, in the foreground, the rediscovered water feature created by Johnston to simulate the glacial melt. It echoes Mawson's maxim that 'Unless water accompanies the rock garden in some form or another it never appears complete.'

To the west of the Lily Pool was a tennis court enclosed by yew hedges, with a thatched shelter on the western side. The court is close to 37 by 18 metres (120 by 60 feet), again following Mawson's detailed advice:

Lawns for single tennis courts should, where possible, have a total length and width approximating one hundred and twenty feet by sixty.

The Plant House, reinstated in the winter of 2003, seen in spring from across the Lily Pool.

One of the last parts of the garden to be created in the late 1920s was the Wilderness, lying to the east of the Long Walk and to the south of the Upper Stream Garden. This originally included an enclosure for birds such as rheas and flamingos, as shown in this contemporary photograph.

The beautiful garden created by Lawrence Johnston during the years following his arrival at Hidcote in 1907 until the late 1920s, when the Long Walk was extended to the south and the Wilderness added, has changed little over the subsequent eighty years. The vista along the principal axis from the Cedar Lawn through the Old Garden, the Red Borders and the Stilt Garden to Heaven's Gate leads the visitor through a succession of differing gardens while the second one, at right angles running from the Gazebo through the Long Walk to the gates at the end, has a peaceful green simplicity.

Right: The Lime Avenue, running east towards the statue of Hercules, is visible straight ahead as you leave the Manor House to enter the garden.

Below: The flamingo pool in the Wilderness in the mid-1930s.

4. Lawrence Johnston and Plant Hunting

In the early 20th century there was considerable competition among affluent garden owners to be the first to have spectacular and exotic plants, and the 1920s saw Johnston become involved in sponsoring and taking part in plant-hunting expeditions. In the first quarter of the 20th century expeditions had been sponsored primarily by commercial companies and nurseries, such as Veitch and Bees Ltd. But in the years following World War I the pattern changed, with individual plant hunters increasingly being sponsored by syndicates of wealthy gardeners who began to club together as a way of sharing the cost and responsibilities entailed.

The botanic gardens at Kew and Edinburgh were also frequently part of these syndicates, contributing 'in kind' by agreeing to receive the plants and seeds collected by the plant hunter and then distribute them to those who had purchased shares in the particular expedition, whilst retaining some for themselves. Each shareholder received plants and seeds in proportion to the payment contributed to the syndicate or, as became more common in later years, received plants and seeds of a requested type or genus.

Another source of plants and seeds of new plants was from fellow members of the Garden Society, which was set up in 1920. At its first meeting, the society was named; it was agreed that the number of members should not exceed 40 (later increased to 50), members must be Fellows of the Royal Horticultural Society – and all must be male (thus preventing membership from the several knowledgeable 'lady gardeners' of the time, and essentially creating a gentlemen's club). The Society would meet at least twice a year and dine together on the first night of the RHS Spring Meeting, now held at Chelsea, and on the night of the first RHS meeting in November. Members would be those 'who not only possessed gardens but were actively engaged in the cultivation, increase and exchange of plants, and especially plants of more recent introduction.' All members were encouraged to bring some flower or plant of horticultural or botanical interest to the two or three dinners each year, and to give a short description or history of it afterwards. This policy of exchanging both plants and information suitably illustrated the Society's motto *'Petimus Damusque Vicissim'* ('Turn by turn we ask and give').

Original Garden Society members included several illustrious gardeners of the day, such as E A Bowles of Myddelton House, Reginal Cory of Dyffryn, Sir George Holford of Westonbirt, Sir William Lawrence of Burford, Surrey, the Hon. H D McLaren of Bodnant, Major Lionel de Rothschild of Exbury and Frederick C Stern of Highdown. Mark Fenwick of nearby Abbotswood became a member in 1921 and wrote to Lionel de Rothschild to ask him if he would support the nomination of Lawrence Johnston 'who is a *very* keen & very good gardener.' Johnston, along with the Marquis of Headfort of Kells, was duly elected a member in a meeting of May 1922. The Garden Society provided Johnston with a network of other leading gardeners, with whom it was easy to exchange seeds and cuttings; he continued to be a member of the Garden Society until 1948, the year in which he gave Hidcote to the National Trust and went to live permanently in France, where he tended his garden at Serre de la Madone.

In fact during the mid-1920s, when Hidcote's development was in its final stages, Johnston, now in his fifties, was already developing this other significant Arts and Crafts garden. He had purchased the villa and land, at Serre de la Madone, a site inland along the Gorbio valley from Menton, on the south coast of France adjacent to the border with Italy, during his mother's later years. By the early 1920s Mrs Gertrude Winthrop had taken to spending the winters at Menton and summers at Hidcote, establishing a pattern that Johnston himself followed in subsequent years.

In 1922 Lawrence Johnston went plant hunting in the Swiss Alps with E A Bowles, a fellow member of the Garden Society, staying at Lauteret, near Grenoble. Other members of the party included Dick (R D) Trotter (later a Garden Society member) and Mrs Garnett-Botfield, who listed the plants collected in her diary. It was a short and not particularly arduous trip, since they left on 29 June travelling by train and bus to the Hotel des Glaciers at Lauteret, from which they made easily tackled daily excursions. From then on Johnston took part in many expeditions, either travelling or as sponsor (and sometimes both), and also visited many gardens. He kept meticulous records of his expenses while travelling, which provide evidence that during the period 1925 to 1928 alone he went to many gardens both in Britain and abroad, to identify and collect species of plants such as *Arbutus canariensis* and *Calceolaria violacea*, for both Hidcote and Serre de la Madone.

In 1923 Johnston became a member of a syndicate that sponsored a German plant hunter, W T Goethe, to visit the Andes to collect plants and seeds from the province of Neuquen, in Argentina. Goethe was originally being funded by A K Bulley of Bees Ltd, who wrote to Garden Society member H D McLaren, at Bodnant, seeking to transfer responsibility for sponsorship to the syndicate. There were six subscribers, each paying £100, among them Johnston and all, apart from Bulley, members of the Garden Society. Goethe was in the Andes during the period from September 1923 until early 1924 and sent roots and plants back to the Royal Botanical Garden Edinburgh to divide and send out to the subscribers. Unfortunately no records have been found of what was sent out, but Johnston was receiving newly collected plant material from Edinburgh from 1923 onwards.

In 1926 Johnston was a sponsor of Frank Kingdon-Ward's expedition to the northern frontiers of Burma, to collect mainly rhododendron seed, along with *meconopsis* and primula. His mother also died that year, leaving him Hidcote Manor, her money in England and the income from her $2 million investments in the United States (with a clause that her estate there was to be divided among his children on his death that was probably a ruse to avoid payment of death duties). With greater wealth, Johnston now had more freedom to engage in more adventurous plant-hunting expeditions and embarked on several.

In 1927, he resumed his travels to collect plants for both his gardens, with visits to the Royal Botanic Garden in Edinburgh for *Melaleuca thymoides*, to Bodnant, and then to the Chelsea Flower Show for *Lewisia finchae*, before calling in at a garden closer to home – Mark Fenwick's garden at Abbotswood – for *Paeonia*

'Sunbeam' and 'Fire King'. In September 1927 he organized a three-month long expedition to South Africa in the company of Collingwood 'Cherry' Ingram, Reggie Cory and George Taylor (later to be the director of the Royal Botanic Gardens at Kew), seeking plants not only for their own gardens but also for Kew and Edinburgh. Johnston, who was accompanied by his chauffeur and valet, arranged for two cars – a Jeep and a Buick – to be waiting for the group in Cape Town. He visited Kirstenbosch botanical gardens in the shadow of Table Mountain and went on to visit other towns in the Cape before going along the coast on the Garden Route. Other journeys were made inland, north into the Karoo and also north from Port Elizabeth into the Drakensberg mountains. Several of the genera recorded, if not the species – such as *Aloe*, *Cotyledon*, *Cyrtanthus*, *Felicia*, *Hypoxis*, *Ipomea*, *Jasminum*, *Kniphofia* and *Lobelia* – are still flourishing at Hidcote.

Above: Johnston (seated in the middle) with George Taylor (also seated) at a camp in South Africa in autumn 1927.

Early the following year, Johnston travelled to Kenya to climb Mount Kilimanjaro. In some of the very rare descriptive passages in his diary, he describes climbing on the mountain: on 17 February he walked to Peter's Hut and 'in the gully found Hypericum yellow' – perhaps the same *Hypericum* 'Hidcote' that now flourishes at Hidcote. Four days later he records that 'the boys nearly burnt the hut down by making too big a fire'. He described the trip in the only article he wrote, entitled 'Some Flowering Plants of Mount Kilimanjaro', published in October 1929 in *New Flora and Silva*. His writing is evocative and gives a good sense of the experience:

> After all, I realized that in all that waste of dry grass and scrub and even of tropical forest, where lush green leaves prevent the growth of many flowering plants, Kilimanjaro has its little flower gardens, hidden in rocky dells, sheltered from wind and watered by streams from the melting snows. The King of these little valleys is *Senecio Johnstonii* … as picturesque a plant as so essentially an ugly one can be. It looks like a huge artichoke of pale green leaves on a woody stem, sometimes as much as 15 feet high, and often branched into several heads. The old leaves, dry and brown, hang down and cling to the stem, making a thick mantle from which the brilliant green tufts of leaves arise. This colour tells tremendously against the neutral background of the rocks and grass. It often grows on a high boulder or a mound with great effect, as if conscious of its kingly dignity. The plant was not in flower, but I secured a good supply of seed, and I hope that, at least in some places, it will prove hardy in England.

> Every step we took over the black boulders of this little gully brought some new treasure into sight. The banks were covered in heather and long grasses, and many Ferns were about the shaded pools. A very fine dwarf *Hypericum*, with slender foliage and large, deep, orange-yellow flowers with dashes of red, grew amongst the heather, and may be hardy in our gardens, as this, too, grows at a great altitude and always near where streams had dug their beds deep into the rock and there is moisture and shelter and hot sun.

> In one place, where there was moisture and shade, were large clumps of a tall bright pink *Orchis* with many spikes in full bloom, but luckily with some ripe seed. I hope that plants will be raised from seed of this which I sent home. It is as big as *Orchis foliosa*, but a brilliant pink and, to my mind, a much more lovely thing.

On his return from Kenya, Johnston wrote in April 1929 to William Wright Smith, the Regius Keeper at the Royal Botanical Gardens Edinburgh, expressing interest in sponsoring a plant-hunting expedition by the celebrated Scottish plant collector,

George Forrest. It is likely that he met Forrest in Edinburgh in May 1929 and, later that year, Johnston, Lionel de Rothschild and F C Stern (all Garden Society members) were all considering whether to sponsor Forrest – who, at one stage in August 1929, became so frustrated that he declared he wanted 'nothing more to do with the affair, at least as far as the current proposal is concerned.' Nevertheless, by December 1929 the planning for the expedition, with Forrest to do the plant hunting, had moved ahead and funding was being sought. In February 1930, William Wright Smith wrote to potential subscribers, saying:

> As you know we are all trying to fix up another Forrest expedition for two seed-collecting seasons. The aim is a sum of £4000. Major shares to be £500. So far we have promises of £3000, made up of 3 at £500 and the others running from £100 to £125. I think the remainder can be secured.
>
> I am enclosing two statements – one giving an outline of the area and one stating the genera likely to be secured. There is no intention of making this expedition confined to Rhods. [Rhododendrons] Seed-collecting is the main object. Mr L Johnston is accompanying Mr Forrest.
>
> It will be Forrest's last venture. We shall be delighted to have you on the list if you would care to consider it.

Johnston was involved throughout in trying to raise the funds for the expedition and was one of the four who contributed £500, the others being Lionel de Rothschild, J J Crosfield and the Royal Horticultural Society. Having been so involved in raising the funds, it is unsurprising that he chose to accompany the expedition, although this proved to be a rather ill-starred decision.

The expedition to Yunnan, southwestern China, began in 1930. It had an inauspicious start, with Forrest already expressing his dissatisfaction with his travelling companion in no uncertain terms. It is likely that there was a fundamental misunderstanding in that Johnston, who had helped to raise the then sizeable sum of £4,000, wanted to go along to enjoy the social life and to see how it all went, whereas Forrest was clearly expecting him to be engaged in the day-to-day work of the expedition. Given the conventional social relationship between upper-class garden owners and their paid plant hunters, this was probably an unrealistic assumption on Forrest's behalf – even though he had by then established himself as a successful plant hunter. Nevertheless, Forrest's unhappiness was expressed in his letters to William Wright Smith:

A recently discovered photograph showing Lawrence Johnston on the Forrest expedition to Yunnan, China in 1930–31.

Johnston had left me to take up his residence with the Clerks, leaving me – as he did in Rangoon – to attend to everything in the way of preparation for our journey, engaging chairs & chairbearers, coolies & mule transport, etc. … There was much he could have done to lighten my labours, but he was too busy gadding around with Mrs Clerk & others all & every day, riding in the morning, tea and tennis in the afternoons & bridge at the club in the evening.

Johnston then fell ill at Tengyueh, in western Yunnan, and Forrest's letters refer to him having Bright's disease – a kidney disease today known as nephritis – from which Johnston's father-in-law and, Forrest states, Johnston's mother had died. Johnston's illness meant he had to return home, leaving in April 1931 while Forrest continued on, with some relief. This turned out to be the last of George Forrest's expeditions as early in 1932, while still on this expedition he collapsed and died of a massive heart attack, just outside Tengyueh.

In late 1931 Johnston had asked the Japanese collector, Kan Yashiroda, about a plant-hunting expedition to Formosa, present-day Taiwan. In a letter of December 1931, Yashiroda thanks Johnston 'for your kind inquiry into our plant-hunting expeditions' and goes on to describe how the plant hunting would be carried out, giving a graphic description of some of the dangers involved:

> I collect employing two or more men of Takasago tribe (ferocious aborigines living on the highlands and high mountains throughout Formosa whom are skilful in climbing on the lofty tree: these savages killed more than 200 people two years ago and still occasionally: they proud very much that their houses are decorated by many craniums of the foreign who were killed by them: very dangerous savages indeed. But such a matter is nothing to me and I can manage. Employing some semi-civilized aborigines who speak the Japanese a little as guide and collector to climb on the lofty trees, I can easily collect.

The costs are then addressed, with Yashiroda saying that 'I estimate the expenditure on the Formosan expedition £150 (one hundred and fifty pounds) including all the expenses (including the expense on forwarding seeds and specimens to you).'

Johnston and five other subscribers – who included the Marquis of Headfort, Lionel de Rothschild and Hon. H D McLaren (all Garden Society members) – each paid £25 towards the cost of the expedition to Formosa, which took place during 1932. By November of the same year the various subscribers were being sent lists of the seeds and plants that had been sent by Yashiroda to the Royal Botanic Gardens, Kew, which would distribute the seeds and plants to subscribers, along with copies of Yashiroda's field notes. Similarly, Johnston sent lists of plants and seeds he had available for exchange to other gardeners, both in Britain and abroad, so expanding his collection. This practice continued until the early 1950s.

Johnston gained two further awards of merit from the RHS during the late 1920s. The first in July 1925 for *Pistorinia intermedia*, also known as *Cotyledon hispanica*, an annual introduced from Morocco by Johnston and described by the RHS as having straggling stems about a foot high, succulent, bearing sedum-like leaves and the flowers are bright yellow, minutely dotted and tipped with red. The second was in October 1929 for *Gordonia axillaris* described by the RHS as being a 'very striking plant producing large white flowers like single Camellias and massive, dark green, narrow oblong leaves'.

5. Hidcote in its Heyday

In the late 1920s and into the 1930s, it was a 'Golden Age' for Hidcote, with the garden now being opened to the general public on two or three days a year, with the admission charge donated to worthy causes – for example, in 1930 it was open, with an admission charge of 1 shilling, on 5 June from 11am to 7pm, for the Queen's Institute of District Nursing. Later the same year on 23 and 30 August, it was opened for the Children's London Garden Fund. The public opening of gardens in order to raise funds for charity was the forerunner of today's National Gardens Scheme and was supported not only by many of the landed gentry, including members of the Garden Society, but also by the King, who opened Sandringham's grounds to visitors.

In 1922 Johnston had appointed Frank Adams, who had previously worked at Windsor Castle, as his first, and only, professional head gardener. Adams led a team of staff who maintained Hidcote in its full glory, and he and Johnston enjoyed a close working relationship until Adam's untimely death in 1939.

The first published descriptions of Hidcote – two articles by H Avray Tipping, the garden architect and horticultural adviser, in *Country Life* in 1930 and one by Russell Page, the garden designer, in *The Listener* in 1934 – give a good idea of how the garden was at this time. Over a decade later further descriptions are provided in articles by Norah Lindsay in *House and Garden* in 1948, an unpublished contribution by her daughter, Nancy Lindsay, from the same year, and by Vita Sackville-West in the *Journal of the Royal Horticultural Society*, in 1949. Further insight is given by the information contained in Johnston's personal papers, – a slim notebook for 1925 to 1928 and his engagement diaries for 1929 and 1932 – which came to light in 2002.

Above: A 1930 *Country Life* photograph of the entrance gates to the courtyard at Hidcote Manor. The camellia house, which no longer exists, is visible behind the left-hand gate.

Tipping's *Country Life* article, from February 1930, is entitled 'Hidcote Manor, Gloucestershire The Seat of Mr. Lawrence Johnston' and describes:

A pleasant stone house, of the type that abounds in the Cotswolds. But the gardens are exceptional. They were excellently laid out some twenty years ago, and are admirably maintained. … solid gates … hung on to urn-surmounted stone piers such as were usual in Late Stuart days. Here botanic interest could easily be added to picturesque architecture. To the right, between ways into stable yard and kitchen court, simple but shapely buildings were given full value, and between their walls and the spacious gravel area there was room for interesting planting. Thus a *Plagianthus [Hoheria] betulinus*, with its birch-like foliage and clusters of drooping July blooms, was given wall protection, but quickly shot up above even roof height to enjoy all the breezes of heaven … Arbutus and other evergreens are less aspiring, but swell out freely over the gravel. Between and among them are spaces for a few choice plants and bulbs, such as the splendid *Lilium centifolium*, which reared its grand flowering heads eight feet high into last summer's warmth and was the most attractive detail of the outlook from the opposite side of the court.

More detail about the planting was given in Tipping's second *Country Life* article in August 1930. The scene today is little changed apart from the absence of the camellia house, formerly along the courtyard wall. Everything else, including most of the plants and shrubs, is still there.

In the forecourt *Lilium centifolium* was only getting ready to repeat its previous season's bloom heads at a height of eight or nine feet, and *Magnolia delavayi* was at the same stage. But the climbing hydrangea (*H. Petiolaris*) was flowering up to the house eaves, and two twelve-foot high bushes of *Plagianthus [Hoheria] Lyalli*, pinned against the wall, were hung with thousands of their large pendant white blooms.

Tipping goes on to describe the east front garden between the house and the road. He passed through a wicket at the north-east corner of the house into a flowering parterre that occupied the rectangle lying before the former front door. This had box-edged squares bedded with lavender blue nemesias and petunia 'silver lilac', from which arose standards of heliotrope, harmonizing with the colour scheme and scenting the air. Tubs of pink hydrangea *hortensis* at the corners completed the arrangement. Russell Page, four years later, provided a fuller – and slightly different – description that showed a change of design and planting:

The courtyard as seen from the Manor House with the old camellia house on the right-hand side.

The same view of the courtyard today, with the camellia house gone.

Top: A 1930 *Country Life* photograph looking west from the Cedar Lawn through the Old Garden towards the Stilt Garden along the principal axis of the garden called by Tipping the 'great alley'.
Above: A 1930 *Country Life* photograph looking from the Gazebos back through the Red Borders to the Cedar of Lebanon.

Four beds, edged with the low-growing variegated euonymus, are divided by cobbled paths. These beds are planted out in spring with silvery-mauve violas, and now with pink begonias and Earlham hybrid montbretias. In the centre of each is a standard silvered-leaved *centaurea* … The wall between this garden and the sunken lane has been lowered and made more architectural by two stone urns. Across the road a wide avenue of limes runs up a sloping grass field to a stone group placed on axis with the centre of the house. So, by simple means, a sense of space has been given, and a tiny garden been prolonged into the open country.

Moving on to a description of the main garden, Tipping reached what he called the great alley running west from beneath the cedar tree:

> A broad central grassway, starting east of the house, runs south of it and up west to a distant pair of wrought-iron gates, and another broad and lengthy way starts out from its high part and runs southward, so that big structural lines, in consecutive and unobstructed sections, give outlook and extent. … Their sides form part of the screens of the varied adjuncts and dependencies – the small enclosures differently treated and differently furnished, just as in a great house a central gallery, of which the pillared divisions do not hinder the end to end vista, may have, opening from it, a set of cabinets and closets for the display of duly selected and ordered objects of art and vertu.

The illustrations to the left, from 1930, show views that will be recognized instantly today. Tipping describes the planting in the main beds of the Old Garden in 1930:

> On either side of us we have a broad border to which length of blooming season and continued harmony of tones are given. Greys and pinks predominate, the first by persistent foliage, the second by successional bloom. Tulips begin it in May, and as they go off *Eremurus robustus* shoots up its tall heads. That best of the *sidalceas*, 'Sussex Queen', follows; while a long lasting summer groundwork is afforded by pink snapdragons, above which sway the feathers of *Tamarix aestivalis*, arch the boughs of rose 'Prince de Bulgarie', and twinkle the stars of single pink dahlias.

Russell Page in 1934 added more information:

Under the cedar tree it starts as a little lawn surrounded by thick squat hedges of box, then it passes between two wide flower beds. …They continue in autumn a theme of pink established in spring by thousands of pink and red tulips deeply planted, pink lupins, and the tall spires of eremurus. Now later pink star dahlias and snapdragons form a rosy foam from which rise bushes of the pink *Tamarix aestivalis* and an old-fashioned rose 'Prince de Bulgarie'.

The structure described is barely changed today and many of these plants still remain.

Right: A 1930 *Country Life* photograph looking from the Circle through the gates into the Old Garden and the Cedar of Lebanon. The semicircular seat can be seen in the distance.

Below: The same view today.

Tipping went on to describe the garden to the south of the cedar tree, which today is the White Garden:

> To the south, a narrow flight takes us to the first of the many enclosures. Here phloxes revel, and the mid-September sun shows their brilliant heads with startling vividness against their yew hedge backing. From the yew arch we look back across the paved circle of this gay little retreat and catch glimpses of the grey walled and many-gabled house through the cedar's horizontal boughs …

Later, he adds further detail:

> … we see down into the little yew-enclosed phlox garden. The phloxes promise well, but as their time is not yet, gaiety is introduced by the Martagon lilies, white and purple, that stand high among them, while the yew hedges and arches are splashed with the scarlet of *Tropaeolum speciosum* which … cannot do better than it does here.

Again, the photographs that accompany the description are instantly recognisable for modern-day visitors since little has changed – apart from the topiary birds having become somewhat plumper.

Above: A 1930 *Country Life* photograph of the White Garden looking towards the Manor House and the Cedar Lawn.
Below: The same view today shows that even the flagstones are the same.

Tipping next described what is today the Fuchsia Garden, between the Circle and the Bathing Pool Garden:

> … we come to where a small rose garden intervenes between the great alley and the round pool. This rose garden consists, on each side of a central path, of a round bed framed by four segments, and is a show of exquisite roses in exquisite condition, the pink Gruss an Aachen exceeding in floriferousness as she concentrates her endeavours at this season and gives very little of a second flowering. Through this we descend the steps to the great, clear pool so still and rippleless, but liable in this sunny season to become an animated Lido on a small scale, where bathers joy in its limpid freshness.

By 1948, this had changed to being a Fuchsia Garden, when Nancy Lindsay described it as having

> … brick paths, and ribbons of dwarf box enclosing beds of miniature ruby and amethyst fuchsias, walled with clipped holly and copper beech, leading to the great raised round pool in its circle of dark yew and box, with great blush-flowered magnolia bushes, opalescent mauve azaleas, rose-pink tree paeonies, foaming creamy hydrangeas, reflected in the still emerald waters where the golden orfe flash …

The Fuschia Garden remains similar today.

Tipping then returns to the great alley to move westwards through the Red Borders:

> From the rotunda we enter the longest of the alley's sections. Backed by tall hedges, a profuse display of shrub and plant occupies the attention as progress is made along the grassway.

Russell Page described them in slightly more detail a few years later:

> straight ahead are two long herbaceous borders planted almost entirely in reds and oranges for late summer colour. Japanese maples and the dwarf mountain pine are clumped at intervals, as is *Berberis Thunbergii atropurpurea*, to subdue too much brightness and offer evidence of skilful and original planting.

Nancy Lindsay in 1948 described these borders thus:

> … down between the 'Scarlet Borders' aflame with the vermillion and crimson and gold of oriental poppies and African pokers, scarlet musk and orange Tiger Lily, Day Lily and Crown Imperial, amidst pyramids of copper-purple berberis, feathery clumps of the silver, russet and jade fox grass, against a towering dark yew hedge …

Top: A 1930 *Country Life* photograph looking through the Red Borders to the Stilt Garden. Above: The same view of the Red Borders today. The structure is unchanged and much of the planting is the same.

Looking through Heaven's Gate towards the Stilt Garden today.

The Theatre Lawn today showing the replacement beeches on the dais.

Tipping then moved to the west between the Gazebos to describe the Stilt Garden:

> There is the refuge of the pavilions, but besides that we find behind them cubed blocks of tall clipped hornbeams that convince you, by their solidity, that they can stand unmoved the utmost Boreal rage.

Russell Page described this area a few years later as having:

> … a pair of charming pavilions. These are small and highly fantastic; brick-built with steeply pitched roofs and interiors tiled and gaily painted, they suggest in miniature all the mannered garden pleasures of the seventeenth century. Beyond them is a slightly raised lawn formally shaped and edged with brick, and on each side are alleys of pleached trees. Then come … wrought-iron gates leading on to a grassy plateau from which the Cotswold countryside spreads away to the summer blue of distant hills.

In 1949, Vita Sackville-West refers to the Stilt Garden as a quincunx, a planting pattern of five objects in a square (similar to the arrangement of dots representing five on a die).

> Nor must I forget the quincunx of pleached Hornbeam, set behind the two small garden-houses. It may not be an exact quincunx in the geometrical sense but the word will serve. It gives a sudden little touch of France to this very English garden. Neat and box-like, standing on flawlessly straight little trunks, it has always been so perfectly clipped and trained that not a leaf is out of place.

There has been little if any change in the Stilt Garden over the intervening years.

Tipping also describes the second main axis of the garden – the vista along the Long Walk.

> You see before you and below you the second great grass alley. High hornbeam hedges frame it. Other wrought-iron gates end it. It is bent, the fall of the first half being balanced by the equal rise of the second half.

Russell Page adds additional details and could almost be describing the modern garden as so little is changed:

> The second main cross vista is axed on the western pavilion. It is simply a wide grass walk with high hornbeam hedges either side. It falls rapidly to a little stream and then climbs again to end far away in a clairvoyee – an iron grille between urn-capped piers. This whole device is in the best classic manner: it gives distance and size to a not enormous garden, and its plainness makes more coherent the intricacies of the various gardens which it separates.

Tipping goes on to comment on the Theatre Lawn:

> The tall yew hedge that we have noticed on our right ever since we left the little crossway rotunda is that which forms the southern boundary of a large rectangular and levelled lawn – like so much else at Hidcote, a well separated item. An equal wall of yew bounds it to the north. East, it ends with a row of great beeches, behind which is the house group. West, it is dominated by an outlook platform. To get the lawn level for games much soil must have been removed from its higher end and much of this was used to form the upper end of the slope into a plateau reached by a great set of steps and shaded by a giant beech.

Since 1930, photographs of the Theatre Lawn show that whilst the beech tree on the raised area has had to be felled, replacements are growing well. The beech trees at the east end, screening the house, have been felled since and have now been replaced by hornbeams.

In the area to the north of the Theatre Lawn is the Plant House by the Lily Pool, which was noted by Tipping as being:

> a large and permanent shelter. It takes the form of a great, moderately heated glasshouse, of which the whole front … [is] removable for the summer season. Thus it … is an attractive resort at all seasons. … in the summer … the whole looks more like a pergola than a glasshouse. If we begin to chronicle the rarities, we shall never be getting away, and so we will merely note two things. The mop-headed bloom in the right-hand bottom corner is a specimen of *Haemanthus Katherinae*, some of which Mr Johnston has himself collected on Kilimanjaro. On the other side, rising up to the roof, we see the top boughs of a fine example of *Gordonia axillaris*.

Top: A 1930 *Country Life* photograph of the Plant House.
Above: The Plant House, reinstated in the winter of 2003, as it is today.

Russell Page describes the Plant House with some enthusiasm:

> Mr Johnston, delighting, as ever, in giving everything around him its highest decorative expression, has done enchanting things with all the plants usually concealed in white-painted greenhouses. His are not white and they are specially designed with a feeling for proportion which makes them worthy of so architectural a garden. In summer, the sides are all removed, exotic climbers ramp half in shade and half in the open sunlight; pots and tubs are hidden by masses of sub-tropical plants; sanded paths, pools for rare water-plants, raised stony beds for succulents, morains for difficult alpines and oleanders set about in painted tubs, all combine to make a very gay museum.

The Plant House, removed in 1955, was reinstated in the winter of 2003.

6. Giving Hidcote to the National Trust

A highly educated man, with an eye for vistas and colour and for well-chosen points of emphasis, Lawrence Johnston's design for Hidcote reveals him as a gifted artist. Indeed, he painted pictures of flowers and a tapestry which hung for many years in one of the bedrooms at Hidcote. One of his paintings of flowers (see page 9) can now be seen by visitors as they pass through the Manor House. No doubt his military service, in which he rose to the rank of major, fostered an ability to organize and command that also came into good use when marshalling his garden employees. While his diaries reveal he was truly his mother's son, enjoying an active social life playing tennis and entertaining guests to lunch and dinner, anecdotes from those who knew him speak of a kindly, courteous and generous man who cared for his staff and made his visitors welcome. But by the 1940s, when he was in his seventies, Johnston was becoming frail. Having habitually divided his time between his two gardens, Hidcote, in Gloucestershire, and Serre de la Madone, in the south of France, he was now hoping to retire to the latter to avoid taxation – once World War II was over.

As early as February 1943, at a luncheon organised by Lady Sybil Colefax, Johnston took James Lees-Milne, the Secretary to the Historic Buildings Committee of the National Trust, aside after lunch to ask if the National Trust would take over Hidcote, without endowment, after the war.

The first surviving document concerning Hidcote's future held by the National Trust is a letter written in April 1947 from Lady Sybil Colefax (1874-1950) to Lees-Milne. Colefax was an influential figure in London Society who is mentioned a few times in Johnston's diaries of 1929 and 1932, and her letter unequivocally confirms Johnston's desire to hand Hidcote to the Trust. She urges Lees-Milne to get the ball rolling, saying:

'Dear Jim, I was over at Hidcote with Vivien Leigh Saturday. Laurie Johnston wants to give Hidcote to the N. T. now. So do get him tied up. You see he is not gaga but has no memory. He told me, indeed took me away specially to talk of this.'

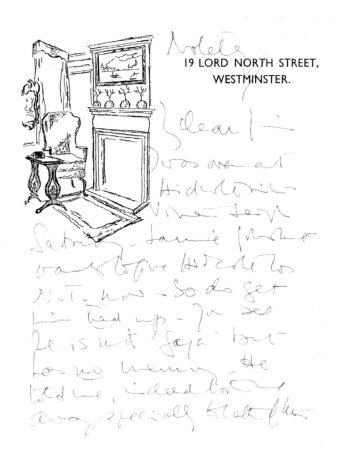

Above: Letter from Lady Sybil Colefax to James Lees-Milne in April 1947.

Lees-Milne acted swiftly, on 1 May 1947, writing to Johnston to say that 'Sibyl Colefax had written me a line to say that … you would like to see me and have a talk about the future of Hidcote some time. I need hardly say that I should be delighted to do so.' He went on to say that he was terribly busy for the next few weeks but would be probably staying with his parents at Wickhamford – about 10 miles from Hidcote – over Whitsun and asking if he might come and visit one afternoon. Johnston replied in the affirmative the very next day, and Lees-Milne duly visited, producing a one-page report on Hidcote Manor, dated 25 May 1947. The report stated that 'Major Johnston offered to leave his property to the Trust by will but wished to know that the Trust will accept it before he made the necessary testamentary depositions.' It also noted that 'the gardens created by Major Johnston over the past 40 years are by garden experts accounted of national importance and interest. Their layout is such that the visitor is constantly coming upon an unforeseen glade or vista', going on to conclude that 'as a specimen of the 20th-century garden, this one at Hidcote is fascinating and probably unsurpassed.' In a final summary, Lees-Milne noted that 'Major Johnston considers that 5 gardeners are the maximum that would be required. He cannot provide any endowment in money, and the Trust would only receive revenue from the letting of the house and the farm rent.' This last point was to become moot in the early years of the National Trust's ownership of Hidcote, which were not without financial difficulty.

Further to Lees-Milne's report, the National Trust began to consider whether to accept Hidcote. The Historic Buildings Committee on 12 June 1947 'decided strongly to recommend acceptance of the devise on account of the gardens, provided (a) adequate endowment was forthcoming and (b) the gardens would be fully maintained and a curator or custodian with proper horticultural qualifications engaged to superintend them in future.' The Finance Committee considered Hidcote on the following day and decided to accept the offer of the Hon. Harold Nicolson to approach Lord Aberconway, President of the Royal Horticultural Society, to see if the RHS could give financial support to the upkeep of the gardens.

On 18 June Lees-Milne wrote to communicate all this information to Johnston, assuring him that:

… the various Committees of the Trust considered your generous proposal to leave Hidcote to the Trust in your will. First of all, I must tell you that they agreed absolutely

HIDCOTE MANOR, CHIPPING CAMPDEN, GLOUCESTERSHIRE.

Major Lawrence Johnston, who is elderly and in very poor health, offers to leave his property to the Trust by will. Before he makes the necessary testamentary dispositions he wishes to know that the Trust will accept the devise.

1. The House.

The property consists of the small house, a stone built Cotswold manor, enlarged by Major Johnston and with every modern convenience. It has three or four principal living rooms and approximately 5 bedrooms (excluding servants' rooms). It is a very pleasant little house but not by any means of importance architecturally. All its contents will be left, including linen, silver, crockery. The furniture is pleasant, most of it oak, but again not of any consequence. But the house could be let furnished.

2. The Estate.

The estate consists of 284 acres, comprising one farm, let to a very good and well-known farmer, called Rightson, from Ebrington. He rents it at about £400 p.a., is well contented and tells me he hopes the Trust would allow him to continue. The land surrounds the house on all sides. The situation on the edge of the Cotswolds, overlooking Honeybourne and the Vale of Evesham, is very beautiful indeed. The village or rather hamlet of Hidcote is included, and is most attractive grouped on either side of a narrow lane, ending in a cul-de-sac. It consists of the farmhouse, a typical Cotswold building in stone, small village room and about 7 stone built cottages with thatched roofs. The farmhouse is sublet by Rightson, the farm tenant. Most of the cottages are service cottages. The village would however presumably be something of a financial liability.

3. The Gardens.

The raison d'être of the property is of course the gardens which have been created over the past 40 years by Major Johnston. They are very well known in this part of the country and, indeed are by garden experts accounted of national importance and interest. In acreage alone they are not large, probably 10-15 acres in all: but their layout is such that the visitor is constantly coming upon an unforeseen glade or vista.

As a specimen of the 20th century garden, this one at Hidcote is fascinating and probably unsurpassed.

Unfortunately, gardens are ephemeral things, unless money is fairly lavishly spent upon them. Major Johnston considers that 5 gardeners are the maximum that would be required. He cannot provide any endowment in money, and the Trust would only receive revenue from the letting of the house and the farm rent

J. L-M.

Above: The report on Hidcote made by James Lees-Milne on 25 May 1947, which led to the National Trust deciding to accept Hidcote.

unanimously, as indeed I expected, that the Trust would be proud to accept the property if they possibly could, for they attached the very greatest importance to the gardens.

But Lees-Milne went on to explain that the Trust was:

… not a little worried about the financial position. It was their opinion that without some further revenue than what the farm rents would produce, the Trust could never afford to keep the gardens up in accordance with the standards required. The wages of five gardeners would amount to quite £1,000 a year, quite apart from the other annual expenses needed for the gardens, the cottages and the house, and the need for a Head Gardener or responsible person on the spot to direct operations.

True to his word, the Hon. Harold Nicolson spoke to Lord Aberconway and the Royal Horticultural Society, but the RHS Council decided that unfortunately it could not accept this additional responsibility. Kew was similarly unable to help. However, in November of the same year the situation changed when the RHS considered the idea of a 'Gardens Trust', with Aberconway stating that he

> … thought that something ought to be done to preserve a few of the outstanding gardens in the Country for the future on the lines of the National Trust and suggested that such a Trust might be established to look after these and other similar gifts. Such a Trust of course would only take over the very best gardens.

Aberconway went on to suggest that this Trust might be under the joint patronage of the National Trust and the RHS and, following consultations with the National Trust, agreement was reached in February 1948 to set up the 'Gardens Section of the National Trust', with the remit to preserve

> … properties with gardens of National importance. Only gardens of special design or historic interest, or gardens having collections of plants or trees of value to the Nation either botanically, horticulturally, or scientifically, would be considered.

This new section of the National Trust would be financed by 'The Gardens Fund', to be launched by an appeal for donations, bequests and public subscription. The properties concerned would be administered by 'The Gardens Committee', of which half the members would be nominated by the NT and half by the RHS.

This initiative was publicly announced at the Annual General Meeting of the RHS on 17 February 1948. Interestingly, this was also the occasion when the RHS, with Lord Aberconway in the Chair, presented a Gold Veitch Memorial Medal to Johnston 'for his work in connexion with the introduction and cultivation of new plants and for the taste and skill he has exercised in garden design'. Although Johnston was unwell and could not be present, Lord Aberconway, in making the award, said:

> He is a great artist in designing gardens. There has been no more beautiful formal garden laid out since the time of the old Palace of Versailles than that designed on quite a small scale, but with exquisite artistry, by Major Lawrence Johnston at

> We are undertaking another thing which should be of value in the future, although it will have a small beginning. Under the National Trust schemes, many of the great houses of this country are being preserved for all time for the nation, but up to the present little has been done to maintain gardens in a similar manner, and with the rising costs of upkeep there is a danger that outstanding gardens may deteriorate and be lost unless some action be taken. The National Trust and the Royal Horticultural Society are negotiating an agreement whereby it may be possible to preserve one or two of them. Only gardens of great beauty, outstanding design, or of historic interest would be considered, and those having collections of plants or trees of value to the nation, either botanically, horticulturally, or scientifically.
>
> The National Trust is establishing a Gardens Fund to be maintained by public subscriptions and bequests; these would be used to maintain any gardens taken over by the Trust. The National Trust propose to appoint a Garden Committee, on which half the members will be nominated by the Royal Horticultural Society, to advise on the gardens and the administration of the Gardens Fund. I am sure that Fellows of the Society would welcome such a scheme, and would agree that the Society should make a contribution to the Gardens Fund and appoint members to the Garden Committee. (Applause.)

Above: An extract of Lord Aberconway's speech to the Royal Horticultural Society on 17 February 1948.

Lawrence Johnston's letter to Lord Crawford, President of the National Trust, saying that the Gardens Fund initiative enables him to make over Hidcote to the National Trust.

Hidcote. Not only that, but that garden is filled, as the earlier gardens were not, with interesting and beautiful plants, some of which he has himself collected in the mountains of China. No one better deserves the Veitch Memorial Medal than our old friend, Major Lawrence Johnston.

The first meeting of the Gardens Committee took place on 23 March 1948. Members of the committee included Vita Sackville-West, the Earl of Rosse, the Hon. David Bowes-Lyon, and Sir Edward Salisbury (Director of Kew). Hidcote was the first and foremost item on the agenda, with the minutes recording that 'the Chairman reported that this property has already been offered to the Trust and suggested that it should be one of the first properties to be considered when the Fund has been raised.' The Committee 'took note, concurring.' Lord Crawford, the President of the National Trust – and also a member of the Garden Society – wrote to relay the plans to a grateful Johnston, who was evidently already looking forward to warmer climes, replying that 'naturally after so many years in care of this garden I couldn't give it up entirely and yet as old age comes on I am glad to live in my garden on the Riviera most of the year.'

Similarly, Johnston wrote to Aberconway to say he was 'perfectly delighted that you may be able to take over Hidcote' but, understandably, was now sorrowful at the thought of losing it. Poignantly, he suggests that 'I could come back here for short periods in the summer. There is so much I have planted that I should like to see grown. For that privilege I might be able to contribute to the expenses' adding, rather more pragmatically, that 'I should have to consult my lawyer about that. It all depends on whether I should make myself liable for English income tax. I could afford to do it if I did not have to pay income tax.'

However, money was also on the minds of the National Trust and RHS since plans for accepting Hidcote were still dependent on raising sufficient funds, and in June 1948 the newly convened joint Gardens Committee – now intent on supporting both Hidcote and another garden, Bramham Park in Yorkshire – launched an appeal with a broadcast by Aberconway and a letter to *The Times*. This letter, signed by all the members of the Gardens Committee launching the appeal, appeared in the paper on 28 June 1948. The same issue included a supportive editorial leader under the headline 'Saving English Gardens':

Today the Gardens Committee formed jointly by the National Trust and the Royal Horticultural Society will be launched on

THE BEAUTIFUL GARDENS OF ENGLAND

TO THE EDITOR OF THE TIMES

Sir,—The many beautiful formal and informal gardens of England are as renowned as the architecturally and historically famous houses to which they are attached. These have had an immense influence on English gardening and indeed on rural life and British character generally, and every one deplores the fact that conditions render it difficult for owners adequately to maintain these national assets. The National Trust is doing valuable work in taking over some of the more historic houses, and now a scheme has been started to save certain of the more important gardens, so that they may be preserved for the nation for all time; monuments, as it were, of English gardening.

The National Trust, in cooperation with the Royal Horticultural Society, has formed a Gardens Committee (of which the signatories are the members) to maintain such gardens and to raise money for the Gardens Fund of the Trust so that this work may be done. Donations to, or covenants for, the Gardens Fund should be sent to the National Trust, 42, Queen Anne's Gate, London, S.W.1, and marked for the " Gardens Fund."

Some outstanding gardens have already been considered, and negotiations for taking these over will be pursued as soon as funds are available. We feel confident that other gardens containing large and valuable collections of plants of scientific or horticultural interest will be offered to the Trust, and it is necessary to make arrangements to maintain these in the national interest. We earnestly hope that all lovers of gardens will respond to our appeal.

Yours faithfully,

ABERCONWAY (Chairman); DAVID BOWES-LYON; ROSSE; V. SACKVILLE-WEST; E. J. SALISBURY; H. V. TAYLOR.
The National Trust, 42, Queen Anne's Gate, S.W.1.

The letter to *The Times* published on 28 June 1948.

its way at a special meeting. A letter on this page asks for help. The aim is to keep up chosen English gardens of special beauty and historical interest, as the Trust already cares for ancient houses. Private owners can no longer keep them up.

> By comparison with Bramham Park it is an intimate garden, although of considerable extent and not lacking in dignity. Small gardens open off a broad central grassway, and the shelter of trimmed yew hedges provides a haven for a host of plants that would be considered dangerously tender for the Gloucestershire climate.
>
> Major Johnston, who brought back many exotic plants from travels oversea, has gathered together at Hidcote rare and beautiful subjects, finding for each a happy setting. The collection of old-fashioned roses and rose species is, perhaps, the finest in the country, and the many magnolias and other flowering trees have now reached mature proportions and would be difficult to surpass in beauty. The formal garden is famous, and the cool, flagged paths of the wild garden lead the visitor through woods where primulas and other shade-loving plants find ideal conditions.

Above: An extract describing the garden at Hidcote from an article published in *The Times* on 29 June 1948.

The grace and dignity of large and elaborate gardens are in danger of being lost in this age when, in gardening as elsewhere, only the great corporation can afford to work, or play, upon the grand scale. Many noble old gardens are today weedy and unkempt.

The following day, Tuesday 29 June 1948, saw a further article under the header 'Gardens to be Preserved', which described the appeal launched on the previous day and stressed the fact that:

Large funds will be needed merely to preserve the best of our gardens from destruction; even greater sums will be required if they are to be kept as members of the new committee will wish to keep them – not merely static but gaining in beauty with the passing of the years.

And continued to specify that:

… negotiations have been opened for the acquisition of certain gardens under the new scheme, and among them are those of Bramham Park in Yorkshire, the home of Lt. Col. G. Lane-Fox; and of Hidcote Manor, the lovely Cotswold residence of Major Lawrence Johnston.

A further two paragraphs described the garden at Hidcote Manor in more detail to tempt donors into opening their wallets further.

At their next meeting on 12 July the Gardens Committee, chaired by Lord Aberconway, decided to give Hidcote first call on any funds raised. As the minutes record, Aberconway's discussions with Johnston's solicitors indicated that the latter (perhaps with income tax liability in mind) were 'anxious that their client should give up his domicile in this country and live in the south of France' and that 'The Chairman considered that there was an excellent chance of Mr. Johnston giving the Hidcote Estate to the National Trust now, provided he could reserve a life interest in the house, and that if this were done the Estate would provide some revenue towards the maintenance of the gardens.'

With Johnston imminently departing for the Riviera, there was a flurry of activity to get the paperwork in order and the deed of transfer signed by him as soon as possible. Letters back and forth indicate the negotiations and agreements involved. On behalf of the National Trust, Lord Crawford set out the compassionate understanding that Johnston should remain supervisor of the gardens for the rest of his lifetime, that the house would not be let and would be at Johnston's disposal should he wish to visit Hidcote, and that while he was at Hidcote the garden would not be open more than three days a week, and even then at Johnston's discretion. Meanwhile, Lord Esher a member of the National Trust's Executive Committee, and James Lees-Milne arranged to visit Johnston at Hidcote on 27 August 1948, in order to obtain his signature on the transfer deed.

By now, Johnston was beginning to fret more than a little about how the staff would get on without his supervision (and, reading between the lines, how the garden might change without his vision). On 17 August, shortly before signing the transfer deed he wrote to Lees-Milne, with a bit of last-minute advice:

I expect to go to France about the 1st of September. I think the present staff in the garden can carry on. I am Head Gardener but they have been here so long that they automatically do the work pretty well & if you can spare the time to come here occasionally I believe it would pan out alright. Albert Hawkins is the only real gardener. He is a great plantsman and cultivator but he has not much head for planning ahead. He also runs a big allotment at his home & I am afraid might give that priority if there was no one looking after him. All the same I was away a good deal & things went on all right. The other 3 are very jealous of Albert but they do their work pretty well but I don't think would stand Albert over them. Of course a young Head Gardener would be best but greatly increases the expense & be certain to alter the character of the garden which is largely a <u>wild</u> garden in a formal setting.

But Johnston signed the required documents as planned, on 27 August 1948. The conveyance document states that:

In pursuance of his said desire the Donor hereby conveys unto the Trust FIRST ALL THAT messuage [sic] or farmhouse known as Hidcote Manor with the cottages buildings yards garden and appurtenances and the several enclosures of arable meadow and pasture land thereto belonging situate in the Parish of Hidcote Bartram or Hidcote Bartrim otherwise Hidcote Barthram in the County of Gloucestershire all which said property contains 261.461 acres or thereabouts and is more particularly described in the First Part of the Schedule hereto … AND SECONDLY ALL THAT messuage [sic] or tenement or farmhouse with the barns stables two cottages outbuildings yards gardens and land forming the site thereof and also all those pieces of land adjoining and thereto all which property formerly formed part of The Hill Farm situate at Hidcote Bartrim aforesaid and now form part of the property known as Hidcote Manor and contains 27.725 acres or thereabouts and is more particularly described in the Second Part of the said Schedule hereto …

Lees-Milne reported back a few days later to Aberconway, with a gentle suggestion that Johnston, by now obviously a rather frail individual, should not be bothered further before leaving Hidcote:

You will be glad to know that Lord Esher's and my expedition to Hidcote on Friday ended smoothly and successfully. Major Johnston signed the Deed of Gift and seemed perfectly reassured by a letter Lord Crawford wrote to him, which Lord Esher delivered, expressing the Chairman's intentions to allow him complete control of the gardens during his lifetime, and the absolute right to treat the house as his own. It is uncertain precisely when he is going, but probably in two or three weeks' time. Meanwhile Lord Esher feels, and I agree, that it would be a great mistake for any member of the staff to go down to Hidcote again in order to make reports or investigations before Major Johnston leaves. He is easily bewildered and worried.

Ominously, Lees-Milne also introduces a new, hitherto unmentioned, member of the cast:

There is another matter that I think you may not be aware of. When we were there, Miss Nancy Lindsay was present; you no doubt know her well. She told Lord Esher and me that Major Johnston had asked her to deputise for him as supervisor of the gardens in his absence. She assumes that this is definitely settled, and it certainly has not occurred to her that the Gardens Committee will even question this arrangement. I think you should know this at once. I have no doubt that Miss Lindsay is a good gardener, and of course she knows the Hidcote garden like the back of her hand, but she is of course very proprietary, and I do not know how well she gets on with the gardeners there.

Aberconway replied in a rather offhand manner, that 'Miss Nancy Lindsay has a fair knowledge of plants – indeed, as you know, she collected some in Persia, but I doubt that she knows much about gardening. However, we shall have to deal with that difficulty as it arises. I am very glad that the matter has reached a satisfactory conclusion.' As it turned out, Nancy Lindsay's presence was a difficulty that certainly did arise, and sooner rather than later.

The letter of 16 August 1948 from Lord Crawford to Lawrence Johnston setting out the understandings regarding Johnstone's future involvement with Hidcote.

7. The First Decade with the National Trust

The completion date for the transfer of Hidcote was, true to British tradition for the sale of farms, the quarter day, Michaelmas Day – 29 September 1948. Once the deed had been signed, the National Trust took over the maintenance of the gardens as well as preparations for opening them to the public on three days a week during the season.

By this time, Lawrence Johnston had departed, taking all his dogs, a couple of servants, a van of furniture and some plants from Hidcote and Kew. Worrying about how things would get on without him, he wrote to Hubert Smith, the Trust's Chief Agent:

> I am leaving here on Sept. 14th for my property in France …
> I think that you will find that the men will carry on all right as they have done for years for me. Albert Hawkins is a brilliant gardener & plants man & has a good deal of taste. He hasn't a great deal of head & has so many irons in the fire of his own that he wants watching a bit. The three others are only labourers but have been with me so long that they do their work automatically. Ted Pearce is the senior & takes the money for all the wages. If Mr. Lees-Milne could come here at odd times I think it would be a very good thing.
> … I think it would be a pity to put in a strange head gardener. He would at once want to alter the whole scheme of the garden which in my mind would entirely spoil it. I hope to come here for 3 months in the summer & of course would look after things if you wish me to …

At this point, Nancy Lindsay re-entered the scene. The Gardens Committee in September 'instructed the Chief Agent that in accordance with Major Johnston's wishes Miss Nancy Lindsay should supervise the garden during Major Johnston's absence abroad', and thus opened the door to a host of problems.

First, Aberconway, as Chairman of the Gardens Committee, visited Hidcote to meet with Miss Lindsay and Johnston's solicitor to 'discuss problems of management'. Prior to this meeting, Nancy Lindsay wrote to Lord Esher – presumably because she had met him when Johnston signed the deed transferring Hidcote. Esher passed her nine-page closely written letter on lined notebook paper to Lees-Milne, remarking tersely:

> I never wrote to the lady, & know nothing of the proposed meeting. I pass this sinister & long-winded letter to you for action. The Gardens Committee must try to get rid of her.

Vice-Admiral Oliver Bevir, the Secretary of the National Trust, subsequently annotated it with the words 'Miss N. is evidently a chip off the old block!', presumably referring to her mother, who was also noted for her forthright and somewhat eccentric manner.

In her letter, Nancy Lindsay set out her interpretation of her role at Hidcote:

> My position is that of a very old and devoted friend of Johnny's [Lawrence Johnston] who knows Hidcote as well as he does himself. Johnny, of course, dreads the idea of any change at Hidcote at present in the garden he spent so many years making. I know his plans for every yard of it. And all last summer he has walked and talked with me about what was to be seen to, what I was to be sure and see the gardeners did. What was to be cleaned-up and cut back. What new plants were to be added, etc. saying 'You must be me, Nancy, and see the gardeners don't forget anything or make any mistakes.' He was very much against the idea of installing a new grand head gardener, who would 'tidy-up' the lush and rather jungly effect Johnny liked. That is at present. I promised

Johnny that I would go over sufficiently frequently to see all his plans carried-out properly, and write to him 'all about everything'.

She added that:

These arrangements are of course only <u>temporary</u>; that is until Johnny returns to Hidcote next summer. … His plans <u>so far</u> are to come over next year for 3 months in summer: perhaps for a flying visit in spring also. … Probably he would come to Hidcote for July and August anyway every year as it gets too hot during these months at the Serre for his comfort. He knows of course that every garden <u>must</u> inevitably change with passing years. Presumably 'one day' the National Trust will install some one in complete charge of the gardens and everything. Johnny quite realized that, and that he cannot expect his gardens to remain 'tranced in beauty' exactly as he knew every leaf and flower for ever, or even for long. But he does anxiously hope that he will come back next year <u>anyway</u> to an <u>unchanged</u> Hidcote, 'altered' only in those aspects for which he left instructions … Some trees and bushes trimmed up and cleared. And so on: I am to see that his instructions are carried-out faithfully 'in the Johnston manner'.

And continued, verbosely, that:

I, as I said previously, am only <u>temporarily</u> a 'faithful watch-dog' for Johnny. If Johnny and the National Trust decide eventually to put a "grand head-gardener" or "bailiff" in complete charge of the grounds, Johnny's idea is that he could 'start one off' himself one summer when he would be at Hidcote for some months, and so able to get such a man into his ways and to get to know Johnny's taste and views on the layout of the gardens.

… At present he says he wishes to keep the gardens 'quite unchanged', except for any 'improvements' he himself may devize [sic], for his lifetime, and will contribute any appropriate costs.

I hope you won't find my 'watch dogging' for Johnny at Hidcote, anything but a help to the National Trust. I am only a 'temporary' until Johnny himself returns next summer. As he said 'You must be my memory and my shadow while I am away' … I would always do <u>anything</u> for Johnny. I hope the National Trust will find me a help and not a nuisance. …

The full extent of Nancy Lindsay's perceived role at Hidcote was news to the Gardens Committee, who must have viewed her presence as somewhat of an unwelcome shock, despite her obvious good intentions. Vita Sackville-West could not attend the Garden Committee's meeting but wrote to the Secretary – presumably with tongue firmly-in-cheek – 'I hope you and Lord Aberconway enjoy your meeting with Miss Lindsay!'

After the meeting, which took place on Saturday 30 October 1948, Aberconway wrote to Lawrence Johnston, sending the letter to him through Nancy Lindsay. In fact, the absence of direct correspondence with Johnston during this decade further complicated the relationship between the National Trust and Hidcote. There was always uncertainty as to whether or when he would be returning each summer, and the absence of any endowment for Hidcote meant that there were concerns each year about the costs and how these would be met. In 1949 there were four gardeners to pay: Albert Hawkins, who was effectively Head

Garden implements in the gardeners' shed at Hidcote.

Gardener, Ted Pearce, Walter Bennett and S Nichols (brother-in-law to Walter Bennett). All apart from Nichols had worked at Hidcote for several decades, and all save Albert Hawkins (who preferred to live in Ebrington) were provided with a rent-free cottage.

Writing to Johnston (and knowing that the letter was being forwarded to Lindsay to read and then forward) Aberconway diplomatically summarized the Committee's thinking on Hidcote's future:

> It was quite firmly fixed in our minds that we wanted the garden to stay as it was, subject, of course, to such minor changes as you might suggest or approve when you return to England.
>
> The garden is a great creation, and should remain an example of what an artist can create with all the plants available to a collector like yourself.

As to looking after the garden, he made a tactfully worded proposal:

> It will be quite a help to have Nancy coming in at intervals with her knowledge of your views, but we wondered if it would help her to have a small local committee, which might perhaps meet once in three months, comprising of, say, old Lees-Milne, Cotton of Kew – a very knowledgeable botanist, and perhaps Thurston Holland Martin, whose views on the vegetable garden would be most useful, and, of course, Nancy herself.

While concerning the role of Head Gardener, he wrote reassuringly that:

> We thought that the matter of a Head Gardener should be left over until you returned. In any case, you would not, I am sure, want to get a new man, as Albert Hawkins struck us as a most excellent and knowledgeable man, and probably you have the same opinion of him.

Johnston did not reply to this letter – perhaps because it was forwarded to him by Nancy Lindsay and he would have known that she had read it. Going ahead with Aberconway's suggestion, in October 1949 the Gardens Committee instructed the Secretary of the National Trust, now J F W Rathbone, 'to explore the possibility of setting up a small Local Committee to help to run

these gardens.' This led to a Local Committee whose members comprised of Major Kenneth Shennan of Shipton Oliffe Manor, Andoversford as the Chairman together with Mrs Heather Muir of Kiftsgate, Mr Joseph de Navarro of Court Farm, Broadway and – last but certainly not least – Miss Nancy Lindsay. Despite misgivings expressed by other members of the Local Committee, and by the National Trust, it was judged better to include Lindsay, rather than, as Jack Rathbone, the Secretary, noted wearily (and no doubt with the possibility of mounds of future correspondence in view) 'hurt the feelings of this tiresome woman'.

The Local Committee met for the first time on 17 February 1950 at Hidcote, and summarized its draft 'terms of reference' as follows:

> (a) These gardens lack a 'boss'. Subject to … the overriding control of the Gardens Committee the Hidcote Committee should, in the absence of Major Johnston, endeavour to make up this deficiency.
> (b) The Committee should … act as a local watch dog for the Trust.
> (c) Although the keeping of accounts for these gardens is not the responsibility of the Local Committee the difficult financial position should constantly be kept before them … and their advice to … the Gardens Committee should help to reduce the deficit that has to be met by the Gardens Fund.
> (d) The Committee is an Advisory and not a Management Committee.

In the end, Lawrence Johnston returned to Hidcote only once, in July 1950. At this point it was clear that all was not well between him and the Head Gardener, Albert Hawkins. Indeed, a distressed Johnston wrote to the Secretary to complain that 'Albert Hawkins seems to be entirely occupied growing fancy geraniums in the greenhouse. They are very lovely but are chiefly indoor plants and don't contribute to the beauty of the garden'. Suggesting that the National Trust could let Hawkins go, Johnston concluded a little peevishly with 'I am sorry to be such a bother but if I am to live here I must be master in my own garden which I distinctly am not now though I made the whole of it.' However, this concern about Albert Hawkins passed, although it was to resurface periodically during this decade.

Colin Jones, the Area Agent for the Trust, visited Hidcote in August, shortly before Johnston returned to the Riviera, and wrote to the Secretary, Jack Rathbone, that Johnston seemed quite happy about everything 'except the fact that Miss Lindsay was on the Local Committee. He said he hoped we would not bring her to Hidcote as he couldn't bear the woman!' Either Johnston had never intended Nancy Lindsay to have such a significant role at Hidcote, or he had changed his mind about her over the years, perhaps in response to her over-zealous 'guardianship' of Hidcote. Certainly Johnston's wish that Nancy Lindsay should have nothing more to do with the house or the garden was unexpected enough to lead his agent, Captain G D Inns, to seek Johnston's confirmation of the instruction he had given to Albert Hawkins 'that Miss Lindsay was to have nothing to do with the gardens or stay in the house.' Johnston replied by return 'I certainly have not asked Miss Lindsay to stay in my house and I should prefer that she should not nor [sic] having anything to do with my property.' Since Johnston's current position appeared unequivocal the Secretary, following discussion with Aberconway, wrote to the Chairman of the Local Committee, Major Shennan, as to whether Nancy Lindsay should be retained on the committee. Shennan replied in a frank and forthright manner that, nevertheless, alluded to Nancy Lindsay's horticultural expertise:

1. Major Johnston has taken an aversion to her. Why, I do not know, but, when I saw him last July, it was the one matter on which he seemed to be clear in his mind.
2. In spite of her exceptional horticultural knowledge, she is only an encumbrance on the Committee as the mundane and practical points which are so important lie outside her immediate comprehension.
3. She belongs to the past history of Hidcote, which we must escape if the Committee is to get control of the future.
4. Professional gardeners should not belong to National Trust Committees, but should be engaged when needed for specific consultation. I venture this suggestion on general grounds, but I feel it is specifically applicable to Hidcote.

The Gardens Committee in November accordingly instructed the Secretary 'to tell Miss Lindsay that she would not be re-elected on the Local Committee for the ensuing year', and he duly wrote to her, advising that it had been decided that professional gardeners should not sit on Garden Committees, and thanking her for her assistance. She did not reply until March 1951, apologising for her delay, and showing a brave face:

It's awful of me. I've never thanked you for your charming letter!!!!! I've been crippled with bronchitis, etc, this winter. Much as I love Hidcote for its own sake and past memories, I can't help being relieved of any share of responsibility of the gardens; as my 'winter health' is sometimes so bad that I used to dread spending days there in the winter. This chronic bronchitis is a maddening handicap!

Meanwhile, renewed concerns arose about Albert Hawkins and his ability to function as head gardener. The Local Committee noted that no thinning or cutting back had been done in the Wilderness for many years, and that many of the rarer and better species were being smothered by less good species. Johnston had initially put in several shrubs of each species with the intention of cutting out some as they grew, but this had not happened despite additional staff having being engaged expressly for the purpose. In the end the Local Committee had to mark exactly which trees were to be cut out or cut back; eventually the situation reached a stage where the Local Committee gave written orders to Hawkins, and then checked that they had actually been carried out.

Lord Aberconway visited Hidcote again in July 1952, when he expressed his satisfaction that generally speaking the gardens were now in very good order. The Local Committee gave instruction to cut back and thin various parts of the garden, and to move the Gruss an Aachen roses to what was then called the Topiary Garden (now the White Garden), below the cedar tree where they have remained.

An interesting development late in 1952 was a letter from Local Committee member Heather Muir saying that G S Thomas (later to become Gardens Adviser to the National Trust) had offered to visit Hidcote to correct the rose labels. This visit took place in July 1953. Subsequently, Muir wrote to the Secretary to say that:

Mr Thomas mentioned that he would like us to remember him if anyone was ever required for Hidcote.

We both consider Mr Thomas would be a great acquisition as he has great taste and knowledge and I am sure could develop the kitchen garden as a nursery for selling plants & sending them to other N. T. gardens. I cannot help feeling that in the long run it would pay the N. T. to have a man like this at Hidcote.

Above: The partially dismantled Plant House in 1955.

Subsequently, clarification was sought from Mrs Muir as to whether Thomas saw himself as a tenant or a Head Gardener. Heather Muir replied that he would like to be regarded as curator and suggested that Mr Thomas could live in the back half of the house without any alterations. But the Secretary responded in the negative, conscious of a possible future need to let the house for further income.

In 1954 the Gardens Committee appointed its first horticultural adviser, Miss E K Field, who visited Hidcote in June and made a report in which she noted that Hawkins does not seem a suitable head gardener in the absence of the garden owner and makes proposals for greater use of the previous kitchen garden.

In the early 1950s the Plant House alongside the Lily Pool was falling into disrepair and consideration was given to whether to repair or demolish it. Although it was initially decided to repair it, lack of funds led to a subsequent decision to demolish it. Sir Edward Salisbury, Director of Kew, visited to identify which plants should be retained in a smaller plant house elsewhere in the garden. After a couple of years of debate, the Local Committee decided that the Plant House should be pulled down to the approximate height of 2.5 metres (8 feet) only, as they considered the building formed part of the plan with the Lily Pool as the centre. But after discussions, reconsiderations and various attempts at rethinking the possibilities, it was eventually decided to demolish the Plant House but leave the back and ends until an extension of the nearby yew hedge had grown up to make the effect less unsightly, and demolition took place in early 1955.

The year 1955 also saw the National Trust seeking a new Gardens Adviser because Miss Field had died in a tragic accident. G S Thomas was one of the applicants, and was duly appointed with much approval from the Local Committee. He first visited Hidcote officially in July 1955, producing a report that gives an interesting appreciation of the situation seven years after the National Trust had taken on the garden.

In a separate note on horticultural matters, Thomas sought to make some changes to the garden. For example, in respect of the Circle he says:

> There are several clumps of *Campanula rapunculoides* in the garden apparently grown for its beauty. It undoubtedly has beauty but it is a most pestilential & persistent weed & I'd like the clumps removed now, during the summer, it will be several years before we are rid of it. There is a big patch in the lilac circle in main vista (showy lilac 'belle Alberta' 1½-2 ft high). The lilacs in this circle have given me much food for thought. I'd like to remove then or replace them with grey foliage beneath as a complete contrast to the red & purple border beyond.

Thomas was obviously having some concerns about how best to deal with Hawkins, and appeared aware that the Local Committee's dealings with him had not always been straightforward. He wrote to Hubert Smith, the Chief Agent, to ask how to proceed, suggesting:

> I'd like to do the instructing of Hawkins, as I rather gather tact has been lacking, I presume this would be in order. Would it be best to act under the Chairmanship of the Committee Chairman or shall I be expected to act as Chairman?

After discussion with the Secretary, Smith replied somewhat evasively that:

> We both think in the first place you should advise the Local Committee and that they should only tell you to give orders direct to Hawkins if that is how they wish it done. Of course there is no objection whatever to your suggesting to the Local Committee that things might go more smoothly if you passed on the decisions of the Committee yourself to Hawkins.

At the Local Committee on 12 September 1955 Thomas's wishes were adopted, with 23 items being listed in a comprehensive Schedule of Work that revealed just how strong a force he was going to be for Hidcote:

Schedule of Work – Autumn 1955

1. Prune young holly hedge along N. boundary of kitchen garden to 3½ ft. x 18ins. and reinforce gaps with seedlings from garden.
2. Prune big holly avenue with long-arm to avoid top branches overgrowing lower ones.
3. Do not spend time pruning fruit trees along rose borders and over gooseberries as these will eventually be scrapped.
4. Scots Fir Garden. Borders to be cleaned out.
5. Acer Garden. Lop evergreens.
6. Grey Garden. Remove ¾ of the Anaphalis and plant other grey plants.
7. Medlar Garden. Thin out medlar. Reinforce base of box hedge with *Buscus*. Lop 2 hollies at corner.
8. Remove Lilacs in Circle. The time for this to be agreed with the Gardens Adviser.
9. Red Borders. 2 Prunus extra. Transplant Acers. Remove Lonicera and Pink Roses. Extra Berberis and purple Delphiniums; Roses Orange Triumph, Frensham; add 12 Red Cannas with purple foliage; *Rhus Cotinus fol. purpureis*; *Lilium hollandicum*; Pokers. Reduce dahlias and limit them to dark-leaved varieties.
1 *Vitis vinifera purpurea* on right house; *Clematis* Royal Valour on low walls.
10. Grass Beds. Retain 1 Buddleia only in each. Remove rampant grass. Rearrange others adding a clump of *Arande conspicus* and *A. donax* to each, also variegated *Eulalis*. I *Vitis* for left bed, encourage these to spread along box hedging and on to path.
11. Rock Garden. Maintain as it is for present.
12. Maple Glade. Transfer autumn and spring bulbs from patches elsewhere. Plant small Vincas, to be cut over once a year in December.
13. Stream Garden. Remove seedling shrubs and reveal stream.
14. Pillar Garden. Remove 2 Lilacs. Add 2 new clematis and 2 from Mrs Winthrop's garden.
15. Mrs Winthrop's Garden. (only one green and yellow plants). Remove Clematis C. de Bouchard and Jackmanii. Slug guard for *Fritillaris imperialis variegata*. Add *Clematis tangutica* and *Veitchii* or *Rehderiana*. Transplant *Paeonia lutea* Ludlowi.
16. Cistus Bank. Cut down Azera to encourage fresh growth, remove Betinospora. Encourage Agapanthus. Plant Cistuses.
17. Pool Garden. Prepare 8 standard Fuchsias. Remove shrubs around Magnolia. Prune *Osmanthus* and remove suckers. Plant ground cover under Magnolia. Plant 2 *Prunus* Kanzan with 7 – 8 ft. stems.
18. Bathinghouse Garden. Plant borders and prepare Paeonies in tubs. Prune some and transplant other Hydrangeas.
19. Camellia House area and little garden. Cut yews and remove odd shrubs and prune. Cut back box hedge. Increase Primula Guinevere.
20. Westonbirt. Remove cotoneasters around Acer grizeum and trim back hollies behind Birches. Plant *Rosa longicuspis* on old dead Pear tree.
21. Propagate *Philadelphus incanus*, putting in 1 ft. long hardened cuttings in open ground in winter (Nov–Dec)
22. Lop Holm Oak from hedge at top of vista.
23. Pot on Geranium to make some good plants. Clear up greenhouse. Get seats ready for summer. Clean out and re-organise sheds.

Thomas's role as expert adviser meant that things were getting done, but possibly at the cost of some friction with the Local Committee. The next year, in July 1956, Shennan resigned from the Local Committee saying that:

> … the circumstances have changed considerably since the Committee was appointed in 1949, as the sentimental reasons which then existed for assisting in the preservation of the garden no longer hold good, particularly since the National Trust appointed an expert to advise on the care and well-being of this garden.

The Gardens Committee agreed to disband the Local Committee at Hidcote, and the Hon. David Bowes-Lyon, the new Chairman, accordingly thanked Shennan for 'the splendid work you have done for us at Hidcote', adding that 'without your help the situation at Hidcote would have been very grave indeed.' Shennan's response concluded poignantly with 'We did our best because of our many nostalgic memories.'

Heather Muir, as one of the Local Committee's erstwhile members, was now asked to help and advise the Gardens Adviser, the Secretary writing to inform her that Thomas should be 'supervised and controlled by you', adding the interesting note of caution that 'Without you this plan will not work because, admirable though he is, I should on questions of taste be somewhat chary about giving Mr. Thomas full control.' Her carefully considered response seeks assurance that her relationship with Thomas is clearly set out:

I should like to continue helping at Hidcote on the understanding that Mr Thomas has been notified that we will cooperate on any schemes for the improvement of the garden, as I would not like him to feel that I am interfering in an unofficial capacity.

Nancy Lindsay briefly sails into view again in 1956, when the contents of the house were disposed of. Lawrence Johnston was by this time too unwell to return to Hidcote, and Mr H A Snelling, his accountant and attorney, gave the National Trust permission to store the contents of the house and to let or use the house as they wished. However, in the event it was decided to sell the contents at a sale at Hidcote in February 1957. Snelling subsequently wrote to the Secretary in some concern over this decision, saying that this sale had caused him:

… some troubles, as certain persons had suggested that a few personal mementoes should not be sold. However, I got over most of the difficulties but I have to refer to you concerning two questions raised by Miss Lindsay.

These 'two questions' related to two plants, golden striped Yuccas, that Nancy Lindsay claimed belonged to her, and to a curious coloured faience Italian lion from the Plant House that she said Johnston had intended to become her property. After correspondence with Hawkins, who could corroborate her claims, the Secretary told Snelling that he could give these items to Nancy Lindsay.

Johnston, through Snelling, had now given permission for the National Trust to convert the back part of the house for use as accommodation for a new Head Gardener. An advertisement in the *Gardener's Chronicle* in September 1956 resulted in several applications, which were reviewed by Graham Thomas. Although

none of these were judged to be of a suitable calibre, Thomas wrote to Hubert Smith, the Chief Agent in March 1957 to say that he had interviewed an excellent candidate for the post. Further to an interview with a representative of the Gardens Committee and the Chief Agent the post was offered to this candidate, Philip M Knox, then aged 31, and currently in charge of a woodland garden in Northumberland. The offer was subject to a satisfactory reference from his current employer, Colonel Lord Joicey – of Etal Manor. By a most extraordinary coincidence Knox had been gardener at Etal Manor, where, in 1899, Lawrence Johnston had been a farming pupil at New Etal – staying with George Laing, the son of Sir James Laing of Etal Manor.

Hidcote continued to require ongoing maintenance and significant refurbishment, with Knox taking up his position there in June 1957. The Secretary met with Graham Thomas at Hidcote in October 1957 to keep abreast of what work was needed, and subsequently wrote to Thomas that:

Seeing this garden through your eyes really thoroughly was a great help to me, and for the first time I really got the impression that we are turning the corner. I like your long term plans and am very grateful to you.

A number of points were decided by the Secretary and Thomas during this visit, subject to agreement with Heather Muir:

1. To fell 12 cedars at end of great lawn; to lop the row of Holm Oaks level with the top of the yew hedge. The hedge must be pruned and mulched to restore its vigour, as it is the most important feature of this area. A further line of Holm Oaks to be planted in the line of the cedars; when these have grown sufficiently, the present row of oaks to be removed.
2. To fell the row of Scots Pines along the kitchen garden boundary, and reduce the holly hedge to 5ft. 6in. in height. The yew hedge to be pruned and mulched.
3. Public access. Whether house is let or not, to allow public to enter through the courtyard and gateway at the end of the house, thus seeing in passing the fine lime avenue and statue, and being able to see the main vista from the right spot, as a surprise.

This final point was a foretaste of what was to be reinstated in 2004 when the house was taken back from a long let and public access could be through the Manor House and into the garden through the east front garden thus arriving at the end of the vista from under the Cedar of Lebanon. Interestingly, in his reply to the Secretary, Thomas was emphatic about access.

Mrs Muir reluctantly agreed with the proposal to fell the cedars and lop the Holm Oaks but argued against the felling of the row of Scots Pines which she felt were doing no harm.

On 27 April 1958, Lawrence Johnston died at his home in France and was brought back to nearby Mickleton to be buried alongside his mother. He had not visited Hidcote since 1950. His will had been made on 20 August 1948, before he left Hidcote. When probate was obtained on 30 October 1958, the value was just over £2,900. His bequests were largely unrelated to Hidcote and included one to Mickleton Church to keep the graves of himself and his mother in good order, and another to St Catharine's

Church, Chipping Campden, the Catholic church where he had worshipped (towards the upkeep of the church as well as for two Masses to be said each year in perpetuity). Bequests of £100 each left to 'my Head Gardener Edward Pearce, my Gardener Walter Bennett, my Gardener Albert Hawkins' as well as to 'Mrs Dorothy Hughes of Hidcote Bartrim, Miss Nancy Lindsay of Sutton Courtenay, William Hughes, Miss Annie Bennett, May Bennett and Sidney Nichols of Hidcote Bartrim'. The residuary estate went to his godson Malcolm Kenneth Shennan, of Shipton Oliffe Manor, Andoversford, the son of Major Shennan who had chaired the Local Committee.

After Johnston's death, the National Trust let the house and had a freer hand to manage the garden. Several prospective tenants were interviewed in September 1958, and a 14-year tenancy at a rental of £250 a year was offered to Sir Gawain Bell, who accepted it and undertook to furnish Hidcote as soon as possible, intending to make Hidcote his home when he aimed to retire from the Foreign Office in 1960.

Above: Extract from a letter of 22 October 1957 from G S Thomas to Jack Rathbone, the Secretary of the National Trust, emphasising the importance of providing access for the public to the Cedar Lawn.

8. Towards and Into the 21st Century

The latter half of the 20th century saw continued financial difficulties at Hidcote. The oversight of the garden increasingly lay with the Gardens Adviser, under the guidance of the Gardens Committee, which now met less frequently – sometimes only once a year in the late 1950s. Even then Hidcote was not always a formal agenda item (although it was frequently mentioned because of the continuing deficit in its costs).

A year after Lawrence Johnston's death, Lord Esher visited Hidcote and, on 17 August 1959, wrote with approval to Hubert Smith, the Chief Agent:

> I went over to Hidcote yesterday, & I should be glad if you would convey to the Head Gardener my admiration for the transformation which has taken place since I was last there. It now seems to me in perfect order, & is as lovely a garden as it was in Major Johnston's day. It is indeed a credit.

He also wrote to the Secretary in similar fashion, and suggested that in some way Lawrence Johnston's role as creator of Hidcote should be commemorated. Esher obviously had a precise vision of what form this tribute should be, as he poetically described the garden, 'a creation which seemed to us, on one of the perfect evenings of this divine summer, a dream of beauty':

> I would suggest, &, if you agree, put it on the agenda, that we should put up a vase … at the end of the long walk where people stand to look at the view of distant hills. Nearly all the visitors go there, & it is the natural place for it. The base should record Major Johnston's name and the fact that he created the garden. I would like to contribute £10 to this idea, & perhaps others in the gardening world who knew him would contribute …

And thus begun the long and tortuous tale of an urn and a plaque. Esher's suggestion to commemorate Lawrence Johnston's gift of Hidcote was considered by the Gardens Committee in October 1959 when they agreed to spend £150 from the Gardens Fund on an urn and invited the Chairman, David Bowes-Lyon, to decide where it should be placed.

As Gardens Adviser, Graham Thomas obviously felt somewhat uncomfortable about the possibility of an urn, and wrote to Lees-Milne on 30 March 1960 to say that he felt

> … very strongly that anyone who is to design the urn should know where it is to go, & in my opinion there are not many places, unless it is placed centrally in a vista, which I should deplore as it would be contrary to the main idea of Hidcote. The only central spot that I can think of where a central feature was designed was in Mrs Winthrop's Garden; this being named after LJ's mother doesn't seem altogether appropriate. It might be suitable under the beeches at the house end of the Great Lawn, or at the east end of the Maple Garden instead of the seat. On the other hand, it might be worth asking the Gardens Committee if a plaque on the house might not be much better in all respects.

As funds were always short for Hidcote, an alternative more practical idea of replacement wooden gates was proposed by the Gardens Committee when they met at Hidcote in May 1961. As Chairman, David Bowes-Lyon, wrote to Lord Esher to tell him of the outcome of the meeting at which 'there arose a considerable feeling that an urn might not be the best memorial', adding that the idea now was to commemorate Johnston's gift by the gates to the entrance which 'should be exact copies of the ones that Lawrence Johnston devised himself.' Esher's reactions to this alternative were sought – but there was no swaying him: however charmingly he put it, he still wanted to go with the urn:

> I would not dream of placing my opposition against the opinion of the Gardens Committee. But I will just tell you what I think, as I would like you to know my reasons for favouring the stone urn. I thought it would look very nice, & attract the attention of the public at the end of the long grass walk, which rises to a sort of summit, & that Johnston's name and gift could be recorded on the plinth. The creator of that lovely garden would thus not be forgotten. The trouble about gates in the modern world is that they are practically always open & thus fail to make their effect. They require a lodge & lodge-keeper, an old lady making a curtsey as she opens them for the gentry. I presume this will not be provided, & they will be always open. Then I consider an inscription that records Johnston is essential. Can it be placed on the stone pillars so that all who enter can read? I hope so. Such are my reasons, but it is not for an extinct volcano like me to stand up against such a weight of adverse opinion.

The Secretary was on Esher's side, and subsequently wrote to David Bowes-Lyon saying:

> Thank you very much … for sending me Oliver Esher's letter to you about the urn at Hidcote. As almost invariably happens I agree with everything he says. Although I am sure they will be a utilitarian improvement I cannot really think that the gates will provide a very worthy memorial for Major Johnston.

But acknowledging that it, ultimately, wasn't his decision

> On the other hand the Gardens Committee were unanimous about this and I am sure that their decision ought to be accepted …

The issue came to a halt, and there was then a delay of a year, until October 1962 when the Gardens Committee invited Alvilde Lees-Milne, wife of James and a noted garden designer in her own right, to visit Hidcote to choose a possible site for an urn, saying that they would agree to its erection if a suitable site could be found. Coincidentally, Lord and Lady Esher wrote to the Secretary – from the warmth of Altamira, Chateauneuf-de-Grasse, in the Alpes-Maritime – and got in a final 'dig' about the urn:

> Please tell that Secretarial optimist how much we appreciated their recollection of our existence. We do not expect, any more than the late Lawrence Johnston of Hidcote, that they will be able to afford a vase when we are dead, but it is delightful to be remembered when one is alive.

The Secretary replied with:

> Thank you so much for your delightful letter … written from your Mediterranean sunshine. I hope to read it to the General Purposes Committee at their meeting on Friday when I tell them that the Gardens Committee at their meeting on 3rd October relented about the memorial urn at Hidcote. Alvilde has been asked to choose a site which will not alter the character of the garden, so I hope now that your proposal about this may be making some progress.

But the search for the ideal urn-related site at Hidcote was not exactly proceeding apace. In April 1963, Alvilde Lees-Milne pronounced that a site for a memorial urn for Johnston could not be identified until a suitable urn had been found. She was accordingly invited to choose both the urn and a site for it, and subsequently made two suggestions for a site – one in Mrs Winthrop's Garden and the other up the steps at the end of the Great Lawn (now known as the Theatre Lawn). After Lord Esher's death, at Chateauneuf in October 1963, the Gardens Committee at its next meeting disregarded both site suggestions and instead '(a) accepted Lord Aberconway's proposal that, instead of an urn, a plaque should be placed in one of the Gazebos, and (b) instructed the Secretary to produce a text and designs for a plaque at the cost of not more than £120 for approval by the Committee at their next meeting.' Alvilde Lees-Milne had been unable to attend the meeting where all this took place and she wrote subsequently to the Secretary in distress at this *fait accompli*:

> I think it is <u>very</u> shocking of the Gardens Committee to chuck the idea of the urn at Hidcote in view of the fact that it was Oliver's idea & that he constantly continued to press the matter & urge one to continue the search. His last words to me were 'Now mind you find that urn for Hidcote.' Now that he is dead his wishes are apparently to die with him. I know this idea was Thomas's as he talked to me about it & I said 'No, no we can't go back now.' How I wish I had been there last week.

Very feeble of you all I think. Jim feels strongly on the subject & is I believe writing to you – something would have turned up in time.

The Secretary, still nobly batting on the side of the urn, wrote to Sir George Taylor, Director of the Royal Botanic Gardens Kew (who had been on the plant-hunting expedition with Johnston to South Africa in 1928), who was now the Chairman of the Gardens Committee following the death of David Bowes-Lyon in 1961, saying that:

> I think we should have second thoughts about the memorial urn which the Gardens Committee decided should be replaced with a plaque in one of the gazebos. The Committee were so unanimously emphatic about this decision, that although you gave me every chance to oppose it, my courage rather gave out! It was Lord Esher's idea. Mrs Lees-Milne says his last words to her were 'Now mind you find that urn for Hidcote.' He felt strongly about it and, now that he is dead, it is a pity for his wishes about this to die with him. Mrs Lees-Milne is sure some suitable urn will turn up in time.
>
> As Lord Esher was Chairman of the General Purposes Committee and persuaded them as well as the Gardens Committee to accept this idea I hope you will not mind if at their meeting on 13th December we tell the General Purposes Committee about this.

Although Sir George Taylor replied expressing doubts as to how the very emphatic decision of the Gardens Committee about the urn at Hidcote could be reversed, the Secretary responded with a last ditch attempt at persuasion, saying that 'although it may cause difficulties, I think we must refer the Gardens Committee's decision against the Hidcote urn to our General Purpose Committee.' It was thus put to the General Purposes Committee who nevertheless agreed unanimously that the memorial was to Major Lawrence Johnston rather than Lord Esher, and the decision for a plaque should stand.

James Lees-Milne was clearly fed up with the whole proposal and replied on 17 December to a request for a suitable wording for the plaque with:

> I think it shabby, mean and cowardly of the Trust to reverse now a decision which they could have reversed during the last

three or four years of Lord Esher's life. I hope at least these words will be recorded. Now for the inscription:

THESE GARDENS
CREATED OUT OF A BARREN WASTE
BY THE GENIUS OF LAWRENCE JOHNSTON
were given by him to
THE NATIONAL TRUST
in 1948.

Getting a final sarcastic point concerning his opinion on the shoddiness of a plaque in comparison with a more noble and lasting urn, he added in summary that:

> Oxidised tin is the cheapest material and lasts quite five years.

His disgust was underlined in a later note about suggested alterations to the text in which he fumed 'Do what you like. I rolled it straight onto the typewriter with no forethought, boiling as I was with indignation over the Trust's pusillanimity, meanness and beastliness to O.E.'s [Oliver Esher's] strong wishes which no-one questioned while he was alive.' Invited to comment on the final 'approved' text he responded caustically with 'I think it is banal and the sort of wording you would expect from the joint endeavours of a Parish Council approved by a cautious vicar.' Further changes resulted in a final form of words:

THIS GARDEN
CREATED BY THE GENIUS OF
LAWRENCE JOHNSTON
WAS GIVEN BY HIM TO THE
NATIONAL TRUST IN 1948

And so ended a prolonged and rather bitter tale of commemoration.

During this time – in-fighting about plaques and urns aside – increasing the number of paying visitors to Hidcote had always been a prime concern. Various possibilities for expansion were considered. In 1960, Graham Thomas noted that there was an open-air stage at the end of what became known as the Theatre Lawn, on which he suggested that the National Trust might persuade local schools or universities, or better still one of the dramatic societies in Birmingham, to produce a play. Alternatively there might be displays of country and Morris dancing. In June 1966, the Theatre Lawn was indeed the site of a Summer Social and Dance by the Birmingham branch of the Royal Scottish Country Dance Society, which proved a great success. In subsequent years, continuing to the present day, there have been on occasion one day events, such as Shakespearian plays, on the Theatre Lawn.

During the latter half of 1958, the new Head Gardener, Philip Knox, had been forced to leave due to illness, and applicants for the post had been interviewed, together with their wives. As a result George H Burrows, who had previously been at Batsford, Moreton-in-Marsh, some 16 km (10 miles) away from Hidcote, accepted the post at a wage of £9 10s. 0d. a week. He was presumably further gratified to find that this was a mistake, and he was actually to receive £9 19s. 0d., in line with Knox's original salary. Burrows, together with his wife and mother-in-law, was invaluable when it came to recruiting visitors as members of the National Trust and their team effort resulted in their receiving an award in three successive years for the largest number of NT recruits at any property. The number of visitors to Hidcote also rose during these years, from 8,122 in 1957 to 20,975 in 1960, two years after Burrows was appointed.

The labelling of plants was also considered. Thomas made proposals in 1959 to the Gardens Committee on this and sought their agreement 'on the desirability of labelling plants in the Trust's gardens which are of botanical interest.' However, the Gardens Committee decided that the expense of employing a man full time to operate a labelling machine could not be justified. Interestingly the Secretary sounded a note of tactful caution in the following year when he suggested to a perhaps somewhat over-zealous Thomas that:

It was good at last at Hidcote to feel that the garden was truly loved and cared for but I do think you must be careful not to overdo the clearance there. You have done tremendous work with the rock garden for example but I think it very important with a proliferation of labels and general barrenness (which will of course be improved as things grow up) it should not look like the rock garden at Wisley. I think we must remember Major Johnston's conception of this garden as a series of crowded compartments, but I realise how difficult it is to achieve the compromise at Hidcote and think that Hidcote, thanks to you and the excellent Head Gardener, is enormously improved.

Tensions between the Garden Committee and Thomas continued. Alvilde Lees-Milne, as the member of the Gardens Committee living closest to Hidcote, was deputed to keep a close eye on what was done at Hidcote and yet the other members of the Gardens Committee couldn't resist offering their individual opinions as well, since each considered that he or she 'knew best'. More than once, various exchanges from members of the Committee sought to reverse decisions taken by other meetings which had issued instructions of one kind of another.

Thomas, as Gardens Adviser, prepared a five-page detailed report, in anticipation of the fortieth meeting of the Gardens Committee, held at Hidcote on 25 May 1961. This report provides an interesting and comprehensive account of the situation some three years after the death of Lawrence Johnston, and is divided into sections on 'Work Outstanding', primarily relating to infrastructure, and 'Work in Hand or Proposed', relating to the garden. The Gardens Committee met as planned, with Thomas's report evidently successfully deflecting them from arguing among themselves about what was best for the garden, since the minutes record that:

Before the meeting the Committee walked round the garden considering points raised by the Gardens Adviser in a memorandum … *(see next page)*

The Theatre Lawn steps renovated in spring 2006.

The Committee (a) decided:
(i) to raise the wages of the head gardener by £1 and the second gardener by 10/- per week from the 1st June
(ii) to thin the Beech Avenue
(iii) that gates, doors and all woodwork in the garden should be painted a colour of blue-green similar to that used at Snowshill
(iv) to fell the Scots Pine adjoining the Beech Avenue
(v) to demolish the camellia shelter and the adjoining sheds except for the long one which should be converted into lavatories
(vi) to fell the beech tree which looking from the house is the right hand one of the group of three on the Great Lawn, retaining the middle one subject to a satisfactory boring, and not for the moment to replace either of those trees
(vii) to prune the lilacs around the Rond Point (now known as The Circle) gently
(viii) to remove the two Kanzan cherries in the Winthrop Garden and not to replace them
(ix) eventually to fell the cedars at the west end of the Great Lawn planting a line of holm oaks in their place
(x) dogs should not be allowed in the garden as from 1962

Even so, it would only be a matter of time before disagreements arose. Alvilde Lees-Milne was first off the mark, in August 1962 writing to the Secretary to say that:

> … I do not at all agree with you about removing one of the two remaining beech trees on the lawn. The gap left by the others is already considerable & all this 'opening up' campaign is to my mind, & others seem to be of the same opinion, completely spoiling the character of that very special garden. I did mention the labels to you ages ago … As to the paint it will soon tone down I expect.

Thomas had obviously overcome any handicap from not being allowed to have a full-time labeller on the staff since the Secretary also wrote to the Area Agent to express concern about 'a multitude of ugly white labels', asking whether these must be white, in addition to expressing concern about the amount of clearing and pruning that had taken place

> … the gardens looked lovely. I do think that it is important for the clearance there not to be too drastic. It is important for the

appearance of the garden like a series of over-crowded little rooms to be retained as conceived by Major Johnston.

The enthusiasm for clearance, and in particular the felling of trees, continued to be a matter of concern for several years. There was much debate about the beech trees at the east end of the Theatre Lawn, which had originally screened the house. Decisions at the Gardens Committee on 9 May 1966 included:

> (i) that one of the beech trees should be removed and the other trimmed and
> (ii) no further trees should be planted but that a yew hedge should be planted across the path, partially screening the house, with openings at both ends, . . .
> (d) approved the narrowing of the yew hedge beside the Red Border.
> (e) approved the felling of the ilex and all but one of the Scots Pine trees to the north of the big lawn …

By this time Thomas was barely containing his aggravation, and wrote to the Secretary in no uncertain terms, to protest.

> I really am very disturbed about the decision taken re trees at Hidcote. It seems to me quite wrong on two counts:
>
> 1. That so small a committee should countermand the decision taken previously by a full committee,
> 2. That such members of a committee who have only been there about twice before should take it upon themselves to alter so radically the garden. That portion of the garden was designed round those trees & I consider it our duty to re-establish trees there at once. Just imagine what the lawn will look like in say 30 years with no trees at either end.
>
> I do hope that something can be done about this matter. Fancy, too, anyone suggesting taking out the bush pine on the Red Border, which has been appreciated as a *piece de resistance* for years by those who know Hidcote. Thank goodness the idea was squashed, but I fear it may be raised again.

With a note of some desperation, he pleaded for protection from this rather interfering bunch of garden experts:

It seems to me wrong too that the Committee should be concerned with the smaller details in our gardens. Is there no way of keeping them to the broad outlines & finance? The trouble is, I suppose, that gardening is everyone's interest, & they like to suggest 'improvements' whereas I think one has to know a garden intimately & weigh all pros and cons before making an alteration.

The Secretary, in a difficult position and, as always, diplomatic, responded with an observation to the effect that all members of the Gardens Committee felt themselves equally 'sensitive' gardeners, and remarked that it was difficult to reverse decisions once made (in other words, he saw little prospect of changing these decisions).

But by 1967 a more pressing issue was how to juggle the need for income with the fact that, as in other very popular gardens such as Sissinghurst, the large number of visitors was in danger of causing permanent damage to narrow paths and grass. This threat to the long-term preservation of Johnston's garden had to be balanced against the considerable annual financial drain on the Gardens Fund: Hidcote ran at a continuing deficit of about £1,000 to £2,000, with additional funds – often of about £2,000 each year – required to carry out repairs and provide accommodation. Budgets often included provisional amounts for repairs that were then removed, either because they couldn't be afforded at that stage or because the work had not in fact been done. For example, November 1967 saw an allocation of £3,098 to Hidcote approved; £582 for the deficit on the gardens and the balance going on repairs to the cottages and farm, subject to approval by Alvilde Lees-Milne (the Garden Committee member who officially kept an eye on activities at Hidcote) of the estimated expenditure of £2,000 on repairs to the roof of the stone barn. Some months later she wrote in irate fashion to the Secretary:

You may remember at the last Gardens Committee meeting I was asked to go to Hidcote to look at the roof of a barn. Well Colin Jones [the Area Agent] duly rang me up & said Jeremy Benson [the architect] wanted to be there too & a date was fixed to suit him. Then later he rang again & said Benson wanted to change so another date was fixed i.e. last Thursday. I have had bronchitis and would much rather not have gone as I have not been out before. However, I struggled up there. Colin was ½ an hour late & Benson just did not come at all sending a message that he had had to go shooting! I was

furious. If I as a member of the Committee can be bothered to go 100 miles on a date to suit him it's insufferable that he 10 miles away can't turn up … He [Benson] is hopelessly slow with his side of the work & I really think should be given a good talking to or replaced. Now as for the rest, the barn is right at the end of the village, but it is a nice big barn & I think for the sake of £500 which is apparently the difference should have the old stone tiles put on again though why the Gardens Committee have to pay I don't see as its nowhere near the garden. Of course the place is in an awful mess, muck everywhere. What the public must think of the N. T. when they go through the village I shudder to think. Then propping up the barn are two huge stone buttresses, lately put there, with pointing of the very worst kind, all hard & square of grey cement. Colin Jones admitted it was his fault as he had not told the builder how to do it. I mean why bother about the roof!

In the face of this outpouring on absent architects and botched building, the Secretary thanked Alvilde Lees-Milne for her 'reasonably cross letter about the barn at Hidcote' and assured her that action would be taken. Interestingly though, this came only some six months after the Gardens Committee had expressly 'instructed the Secretary to ensure that architects were not in general employed for garden or farm buildings' in regard to Hidcote.

Financial difficulties continued in subsequent years but circumstances improved in the early 21st century, when the numbers of annual visitors increased to over 100,000, enabling Hidcote to become a self-financing property for the first time. Today, all money spent by visitors remains at Hidcote and is used to meet expenses and repairs. In 2002 an anonymous donor gave £250,000 for a five-year programme, subject to matched funding being raised by the National Trust. This donation and the matched funding enabled a number of features in the garden to be reinstated:

a. In the winter of 2002–3, the Bathing Pool Garden was renovated, the circular seat on the Cedar Lawn reinstated and the brickwork in Mrs Winthrop's Garden replaced.
b. In 2003–4, part of the Plant House adjacent to the Lily Pool was reinstated and appropriate plants installed, the Alpine Terrace and its removable roofing were reinstated and the Terrace and Pillar Garden replanted.

These improvements were significant steps towards the restoration of Hidcote as it was in its heyday in the 1930s. The property has also benefited immensely from an enthusiastic team led by Mike Beeston as Property Manager since 2001 and Glyn Jones as Head Gardener since 2000. There are currently eight full-time gardeners employed at Hidcote, assisted by some 30 volunteer gardeners. In addition, around 20 volunteers act as stewards in the garden, providing visitor information on the garden and its history.

A further donation of £1.6 million was given by the same anonymous donor in 2005 in order to fund a six-year programme of further reinstatements and improvements, again provisional on the amount being matched by funding.

The house was taken back from a long let in 2004, enabling visitors to enter through the ground floor of the house and then enter the garden under the Cedar of Lebanon in the Old Garden, providing the opportunity to see the vista through the Stilt Garden to the west. During early 2006 the Rock Bank was renovated and replanted and the steps up to the dais on the Theatre Lawn were renovated. The following winter (2006–7) the east Front Garden was reinstated by restoring the parterre of variegated euonymus and the cobbled paths.

Plans for future work include:
2008: Renovation of the Bulb Slope, reinstatement of the remainder of the Plant House, restoration of the Tennis Court.
2007–10: Renovation and replanting of areas in the Stream Garden and the Wilderness.
2009: Reinstatement of the vegetable garden in the Kitchen Garden.
2009–10: Renovation of the Rose Walk in the Kitchen Garden.

With such a programme of restoration there is little doubt that Hidcote will be again in a situation close to that of its heyday within a few years, and the future for this most beautiful garden is bright. Today admission fees from some 130,000 or so annual visitors help to contribute to maintaining the garden, so preserving for ever – for everyone – the beauty that Lawrence Johnston created in the years between 1907 and 1948.

The Bathing Pool Garden in winter.

Tour of the Garden

by Anna Pavord

There is no set route round Hidcote, which new visitors occasionally find disconcerting. Think of it instead as intriguing. There are secrets to be discovered here, which no garden, parading itself openly on a plain, can ever offer. There is actually an innate logic in the way that Hidcote is laid out, with two great corridors stretching out at right angles to each other. One runs roughly west from the old cedar tree by the house, through the Old Garden, the Circle, the Red Borders and the Stilt Garden to finish in the great view through wrought-iron gates over the Vale of Evesham. The second runs roughly south from the summer-houses through long straight hedges of hornbeam to the gate set on the horizon of the garden, which looks as though it might be the end of the world. Rooms, as in a house, open off the corridors, but these are formed from walls of yew and box, copper beech and hornbeam. You are offered more exits and entrances than you are in a house, and the whole is open to shifting patterns of light and shade and the different moods wrought by seasonal patterns of growth and decay.

In visiting a garden as intricate as Hidcote, the long view is as important as the short. Plants are only one element in a good garden and good groupings of plants only one of the delights that Hidcote has to offer. It is only when you lift your head up from what is on the ground and take note of the wider context of the garden that all its elaborate pieces start to come together. Walk to the end of the lime bower and glimpse the view over the stream to The Wilderness beyond. Stand on the curved flight of steps just below Mrs Winthrop's Garden and see how cleverly the garden invites you over the Long Walk, through the tall hedge and gives you just a whisper of what is happening in the Pillar Garden beyond. Most modern gardeners understand plants better than design, but even the most beautiful plant shines brighter in the right setting.

There is also an increasing demand on the part of garden visitors for colour in all parts of a garden and at all seasons. This is not a preoccupation that Johnston shared. Plants had to offer more than colour to find a place in his affections. Overall form, and habit of growth, the shape and texture of a plant's leaves, its scent and – it must be said – its rarity, were all important considerations. And he would not have expected all parts of the garden to be singing equally loudly through spring, summer and autumn. It was a luxury available to those who gardened on this scale (Hidcote covers 10 acres) that certain areas could be devoted to mass displays that peaked at different times of the year. The Fuchsia Garden at Hidcote is an example of this sort of spectacle. Only the most contrary of visitors will expect a fuchsia garden to be at its best in May.

In planting for the future, the National Trust not only restricts itself to the varieties in the garden in Johnston's day, but also continues to plant in the spirit and style that he created. It seeks to develop Hidcote within the architectural framework he established, trying out new plants and new ideas which are in sympathy with his aims.

The tours that follow are arranged in three separate sections. The spring tour covers the months of April and May, the summer tour concentrates on the special effects of June, July and August, and the autumn tour encompasses the months of September and October. The numbers against each area correspond with the numbers on the map on the next two pages.

The Beech Avenue seen
through the wrought-iron
gateway on the north side
of the Theatre Lawn.

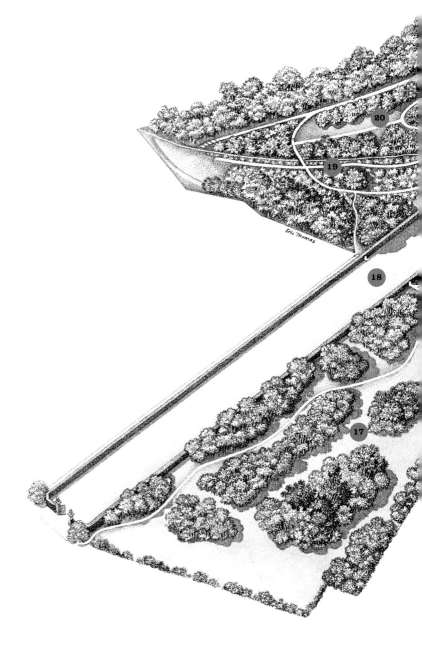

Tour of the Garden

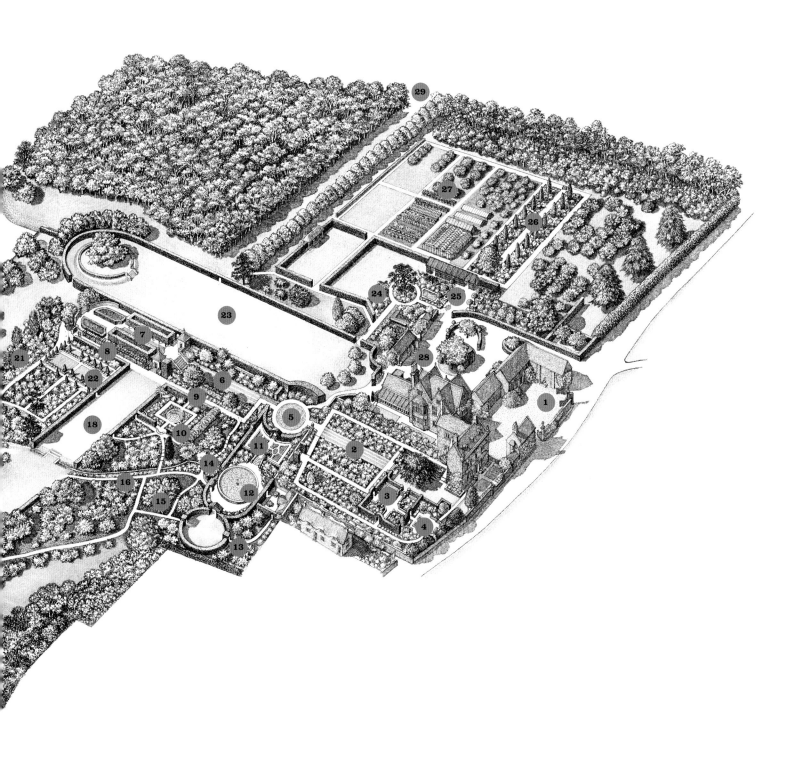

1 THE COURTYARD

The space is enclosed by the house and the range of handsome barns. In the corner is a imposing large-leaved *Magnolia delavayi*, a slightly tender species from Yunnan. It grows with an equally good foliage plant, *Mahonia lomariifolia*, underplanted with pale pink bergenias. New shoots of peonies will be already showing in the bed against the boundary wall, where a large bush of osmanthus shelters the handsome spiky grey foliage of a red hot poker, *Kniphofia caulescens*. A blue *Clematis alpina* spreads itself over the wall of the small chapel through the schizophragma next to it. On the south wall *Viburnum x burkwoodii* is in full blossom by mid-April, but you will have to wait until May for the full glory of the wisteria trained over the exit from the shop and on the boundary

wall. By late May too the fine old rose 'Gloire de Dijon' will already be flowering against the wall of the house. In the border between the two gates there is also a good display from the early rose 'Cantabrigiensis' with masses of pale creamy flowers on graceful stems.

2 THE OLD GARDEN

Upon leaving the house you enter the east front garden reinstated in the winter of 1006/7 from which a glimpse can be seen of the statue of Hercules at the end of the avenue of lime trees. As you turn right towards the semi-circular seat you get the first view of the magnificent vista through the heart of the garden towards Heaven's Gate and beyond. The space, bounded by old brick

walls, is divided into five long mixed borders, the two centre ones divided by a grass path ten feet (three metres) wide. The side border under the house wall has mixed narcissus and *Lathyrus vernus*. Later, towards the end of May, brilliant blue anchusa and white oriental poppies fill the border, and the blue and orange theme is kept going the whole of the summer with a changing cast of flowers. Spread-eagled against the brick wall behind this border is the early flowering 'Lawrence Johnston' rose, raised in France in 1923. The semi-double flowers are a rich peach yellow with a pink flush on the outside of the buds.

A variety of tulips fills the two centre borders, with mounds of pink weigela and pink deutzia behind. When the tulips are gone, the vivid magenta geranium, *G. psilostemon*, covers the gaps,

contrasting well with thalictrum and the pale mauve, almost grey floribunda rose 'Lavender Pinocchio', growing in a corner by the grass path. There are peonies – one of Johnston's favourite plants – including the brilliant pink single variety 'China Rose'. In the shady beds under the cedar, grape hyacinths and scillas jostle with blue *Anemone blanda* and the small purple-leaved violet.

In the narrow border under the cottage on the far side of the Old Garden where Johnston created special soil to grow acid-loving plants, erythroniums, cyclamen and *Bergenia ciliata* grow in the shade of the wall. Hellebores and blue *Anemone blanda* make a carpet under the big *Magnolia sinensis*. There are brilliant blue meconopsis and a collection of smaller rhododendrons, including 'Blue Tit' and *R. augustinii*.

Tulipa 'Negrita' and 'Pink Diamond' in view across the Old Garden to the gates leading to the Circle.

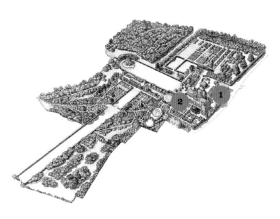

Tour of the Garden

3 THE WHITE GARDEN

This symmetrical little enclosure with its matching pairs of coy, stylised topiary birds is a pleasure to be in at any time of the year. The structure is satisfying and the texture of the box which edges the four corner beds contrasts well with the warm, worn tones of the stone paving. The pale-leaved dead nettle *Lamium maculatum* 'White Nancy' and white violas scramble around under *Tulipa* 'White Triumphator' and artemisia. Acanthus and cabbagey *Crambe cordifolia* make strong mounds of foliage.

Newly clipped hedges in the White Garden (May).

Tulipa 'White Triumphator' and topiary birds in the
White Garden (May).

4 THE MAPLE GARDEN

By the beginning of May the maples (*Acer palmatum dissectum*) that give the garden its name make soft, feathered mounds of bronze, contrasting well with the shiny, chunky foliage of *Choisya ternata* nearby. The two long thin centre beds are filled with fat blue hyacinths and in the raised beds either side you will find *Magnolia stellata* and pale mauve and white rhododendrons, which take over as the magnolia is finishing. A gravel path leads you past a sunken stream with lush clumps of skunk cabbage and wands of Solomon's seal. On your right as you leave the Maple Garden is a fine tall *Staphylea holocarpa rosea* which was introduced to this country from China the year after Johnston came to Hidcote. The clusters of small pink flowers appear before the leaves are fully grown.

Spring bulb display in the Maple Garden (April).

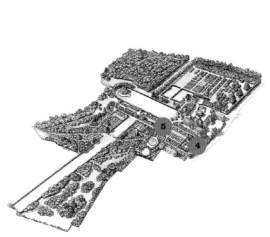

5 THE CIRCLE

The cool grass roundel is surrounded by beds of Rouen lilac (*Syringa x chinensis*), in full flower by the beginning of May. Hellebores and the invaluable perennial pea (*Lathyrus vernus*) cover the ground underneath with a random sprinkling of yellow and orange Welsh poppies.

Yellow and orange Welsh poppies in the Circle (late May).

6 THE RED BORDERS

These are at their height in summer when tender exotics such as cordyline and canna emerge from their winter hibernation under glass, but there is much to enjoy in spring too. In April there is the blossom of different cherries, *Prunus spinosa* 'Purpurea' with *P. x cistena* and *P. cerasifera* 'Pissardii'. Pools of purple sage contrast with the extraordinary orange bells of *Fritillaria imperialis*, each spike topped with a pineapple tuft of leaves. Red-flowered pulmonaria carpets the ground where later roses will bloom and the huge rhubarb leaves of *Rheum palmatum* 'Atrosanguineum' glisten in sun or rain. By May mass plantings of tulips dominate the borders, crimson and deep purple. The darkest is 'Queen of Night', springing from mounds of heuchera. Bulk in the borders comes from the purple foliage of the cherries, a purple filbert (*Corylus maxima* 'Purpurea') and a Norway maple (*Acer platanoides* 'Crimson King'), but by the end of May the tall-flowering spikes of the rheum and some staggering oriental poppies 'Beauty of Livermere' steal the show. The poppies are particularly good with the spiky foliage of bronze cordylines, which are introduced into the Red Borders as the weather warms up. They are plunged in the ground in their pots. If they are planted out, the root systems develop so extensively they cannot be dug up and repotted in winter. But plunging brings its own problems. The cordylines dry out more quickly than plants with a free root run and need special care with watering.

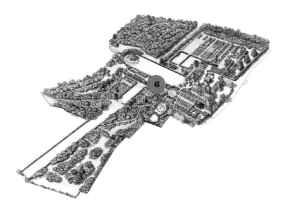

Red Borders in late spring with *Tulipa* 'Red Shine', looking towards the Gazebos and the Stilt Garden.

Rheum palmatum 'Atrosanguineum' in the
Red Border (May).

Lily-flowered 'Red Shine' tulips in the
Red Border (May).

THE STILT GARDEN

Helleborus corsicus flourishes in the small beds round the pavilions, contrasting with the *Hosta sieboldiana elegans*. Spires of the yellow crown imperial 'Lutea Maxima' dominate the end beds with the foliage of pampas and giant grasses such as *Stipa gigantea* and *Miscanthus sinensis*. By the end of May the stiffly formal blocks of the hornbeam stilts will be bright with new foliage.

THE ALPINE TERRACE

These raised beds are protected by big glass covers, which are removed in summer. Just as Johnston did, the present garden team are able to grow and trial rare alpines and succulents that need a drier winter than is to be had in Gloucestershire. The terrace, replanted in 2004, is arranged on two levels with a range of plants from brightly coloured lewisia, the cushions of Draba and the South African Rhodohypoxis.

THE WINTER BORDER

A tall cube of evergreen ilex, Johnston's substitute for the olives of the South of France, nudges against the pavilion. This and the mounds of low-growing *Mahonia aquifolium* provide a year-round foliage background for the more transient tenants of this border. The handsome tree that dominates it is a pink-flowered *Magnolia campbellii*, slow to come into flower but, when it is established, one of the finest of all the big magnolias. The pale pink *Rhododendron yunnanense*, like all rhododendrons, needs lime-free soil, which Johnston went to great lengths to provide in particular borders.

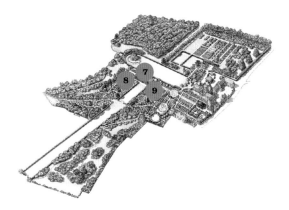

The hornbeams in the Stilt Garden.

10 MRS WINTHROP'S GARDEN

Dark blue and yellow is the theme in this garden, with golden creeping Jenny (*Lysimachia nummularia* 'Aurea') in the low beds and golden hop (*Humulus lupulus aureus*) climbing through tripods in the corners. More yellow comes from leopard's bane (*Doronicum* 'Miss Mason') and, later in May, big clumps of day lilies (*Hemerocallis flava*). Blue spreads from violas growing amongst the creeping Jenny and variegated comfrey. The leaves of the battered Chusan palms (another Mediterranean touch) rustle like brittle ghosts. The boundaries are borrowed from other features: the lime from the lime bower; the beech from the long hedge that runs parallel with the Terrace and the Winter Border; and the hornbeam from the Long Walk.

11 THE FUCHSIA GARDEN

Blue scillas grow thickly in the beds where the fuchsias will flourish in the summer. Dark purple tulips flower in the wall border. Neatly clipped topiary birds frame the entrance to the Bathing Pool Garden.

The box-edged borders of the Fuchsia Garden are planted with blue scillas in spring. Topiary birds flank the entrance to the Bathing Pool Garden beyond.

12 THE BATHING POOL GARDEN

The yew hedge dominates three sides of this garden with its strictly Palladian portico surmounting the semicircular flight of steps to the quiet roundel beyond. The area is restrained in its planting. Fine shuttlecock ferns (*Matteuccia struthiopteris*) and skunk cabbage flourish under the big magnolia, *M. x soulangeana*. In the courtyard with its thatched loggia, big pots contain stag's horn sumachs (*Rhus typhina laciniata*) and blue-leaved hostas.

13 THE POPPY GARDEN

Hostas (the narrow-leaved *H. lancifolia* and *H. ventricosa*) mixed with hellebores make a thick carpet under tall specimens of *Hydrangea villosa* and the strange pink bracts hanging from *Cornus florida rubra*. Blue camassias poke through the undergrowth in early May. The narrow curving path of creamy stone set on edge is particularly pleasing, flanked bossily by the foliage of the hostas. Young *Prunus* 'Kanzan' will in time frame the yew portico which can be seen from the Bathing Pool Garden.

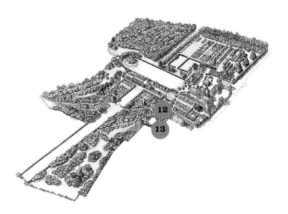

The boy and dolphin fountain in the
Bathing Pool Garden.

14, 16, 19 THE STREAM GARDEN

In contrast with the severely geometric layout of the rest of the garden, the Stream Garden, a large area lying either side of the Long Walk, is charmingly informal. Meandering paths take you along the stream or across to The Wilderness or up to Mrs Winthrop's Garden. From the lower part of the Stream Garden, you can wander in a wide loop up the Bulb Slope to the Rock Bank by the Pillar Garden. It is perhaps at its best in spring, with clouds of blue-flowered brunnera, trilliums, the vivid yellow spathes of skunk lily and some elegant stands of fern. The texture of the Cotswold stone paths is exactly right for this area. They are not the easiest to walk on, but nothing else would do as well.

Blue-flowered comfrey hugs the bank in the Lower Stream Garden, where ground cover jostles under the shrubs. Epimediums give way to the handsome leaves of the variegated

Arum italicum pictum. The architectural bronze foliage of rodgersia (*R. pinnata* 'Superba') spreads like torn umbrellas over primulas and periwinkle. Daffodils and brunnera carpet the ground under a handsome *Magnolia denudata.* Mauve rhododendrons and apricot-orange azaleas flourish in the specially made-up soil along the stream banks. As the azaleas begin to fade, stout magenta primulas take their place.

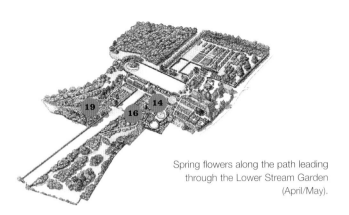

Spring flowers along the path leading
through the Lower Stream Garden
(April/May).

17 THE WILDERNESS

The Wilderness, previously sometimes referred to as Westonbirt, was planned to encourage wild feeding birds into the garden. Cherry blossom and the shrimp-pink new foliage of maples are the chief pleasures of this area in April. The most brilliant pink foliage comes from *Acer pseudoplatanus* 'Brilliantissimum'. Before leaves begin fully to camouflage the trees, you can give the handsome bark of the birches and the maples the attention it deserves. *Acer griseum* has bark that peels in cinnamon strips from the trunk. *Acer grosseri hersii* has bark striped green and white, like a snake. The flat-topped cherry with wide-spreading branches and clusters of double white flowers is *Prunus* 'Shimidsu-zakura'.

18 THE LONG WALK

The bold vista is Hidcote's antidote to the tightly packed busyness of the garden rooms grouped either side of it. The dip down to the stream and the rise the other side give the Long Walk a drama it would otherwise lack. You are pulled on towards the tall brick pillars and their pineapple-shaped urns to see what lies on the other side. The view is intensely rural: ploughland, coppice, pasture. When one turns back to look inward, the brick pavilions with their neatly swept-up roofs fill the foreshortened vista.

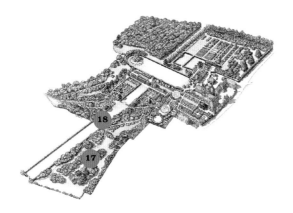

Rodgersia pinnata 'Superba'.

The Long Walk looking east between the hornbeam hedges.

20 THE BULB SLOPE

The effect here is wild, naturalistic and the area is at its best in April and May with sheets of starry blue periwinkle (*Vinca major* 'Oxyloba'), white and pale blue wood anemones, white honesty, Solomon's seal, daffodils and, later, tall white camassias. Hellebores, as always, provide strong clumps of foliage under the groves of young birch.

21 THE ROCK BANK

This long mound of rock and scree was reinstated during the winter of 2006/7 and is being replanted back to Johnston's original design. The scree garden was planted during spring 2003 with bright coloured specie tulips, eyecatching *Pulsatilla vulgaris* and the outstanding blue of the *Gentiana clusii*. The area containing the rock strata is being replanted with sea hollies, great ferns and irises to name but a few. Near the top of the mound on its western edge, a grove of gaunt-stemmed *Aralia elata*, the angelica tree, breaks into leaf by the beginning of May. The Golden Rose of China, *R. hugonis*, introduced into this country only eight years before Johnston cameto Hidcote, is by May already covered in pale primrose yellow flowers. The rose 'Hidcote Gold' is equally early, but has brighter yellow flowers and broader, wedge-shaped thorns on its stems. Both roses have attractive ferny foliage.

By the end of May, pale white, cream and pink brooms are flowering on the Rock Bank with mats of perennial wallflower in shades of mauve and orange. Yellow and white potentillas are draped over the rocks with grey-leaved dorycnium and the dwarf *Hebe pinguifolia* 'Pagei'. A navelwort, *Omphalodes cappadocica* from Turkey, spreads mats of bright azure blue flowers over the bank in May.

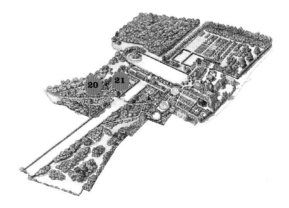

Narcissus actaea on the Bulb Slope and lower Pillar Garden.

22 THE PILLAR GARDEN

This is not to be missed in mid-May, when the peonies are at their best. You can see the bronze shoots already pushing through the ground in April, providing a backdrop for grape hyacinths and narcissus. Huge blowsy tree peonies 'Souvenir de Maxime Cornu' grow on the top level of the Pillar Garden. In the middle section, between the rows of pillars, you will find *Paeonia arietina* with single pink flowers, together with a paler version of the same species

'Mother of Pearl' and 'Avant Garde'. The borders of pink double peonies 'Mutabilis Plena', running down towards the stream, are slightly later than the singles and are a stunning spectacle in late May. Thick purple ribbons of giant alliums (*A. giganteum*) are massed behind them, fuzzy spheres of purple balanced on four-foot stems. The tall thin spires of 'Amanogawa' cherries are underplanted with mounds of the geranium 'Johnson's Blue' and

Allium afluatense and *Paeonia peregrina* in the Pillar Garden (May).

The Pillar Garden with its yew pillars looking towards the hornbeams of the Stilt Garden.

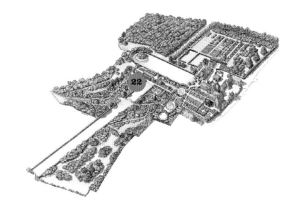

aquilegias. A beautiful large specimen of *Magnolia denudata*, flowering in early spring, spreads its branches over a carpet of herbaceous geraniums and orange poppies. Period narcissus including 'Actaea', 'Flower Record' and 'La Riante' provide spectacular drifts of colour in the lower borders of the Pillar Garden.

Aquilegia and *Paeonia peregrina* in the
Pillar Garden.

Paeonia 'Mother of Pearl' at the base of one of the
yew pillars in the Pillar Garden.

23 THE THEATRE LAWN

This and the Long Walk are the two lungs in the Hidcote garden, the two spaces where the human form is reduced to a completely different scale. Several young beech trees have been planted on the dais at the end of the lawn to replace an earlier single beech tree. The four hornbeams at the restaurant end were planted to replace earlier beeches. A beautifully clipped yew hedge surrounds the lawn, making a semicircular apse at the end. Tall ilex oaks, planted by Johnston to remind him of the olive trees of the Mediterranean, sling a further screen round the lawn. On the right-hand side, a narrow opening leads through to a wrought-iron gate and a long Beech Avenue.

The Theatre Lawn looking west towards the dais and steps.

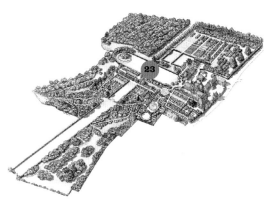

The Theatre Lawn looking towards the Manor House.

24 THE PINE GARDEN AND LILY POOL

Pale pink cistus and the double yellow helianthemum 'Jubilee' fill the small raised circular bed. The newly planted bay trees in the oak Versailles cases once again embellish this area as they did in Johnston's time. The laurels, being hardy, are easier to manage. The pool has low mounds of grey foliage around it and, in early May, the beautiful acid yellow blooms of *Paeonia mlokosewitschii*. By the end of May huge spiky agaves are brought out from their winter shelters and set in pots round the pool.

25 THE PLANT HOUSE

Beyond the pool stands the Edwardian-style Plant House, filled with exotic and tender plants including the striking Brugmansia (Angels Trumpets) from Peru and Pomegranates from Asia. Citrus plants growing in the majolica pots add to the spring display.

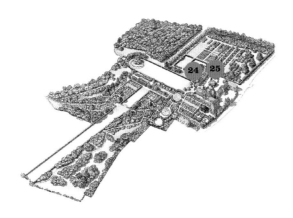

The Plant House.

Either side of the entrance are clumps of *Viburnum rhytidophyllum* with handsome, evergreen leaves, the undersides covered with a buff-coloured down. Tall pillars of Irish yew provide a backdrop for the borders which will later be filled with the smell of roses. In spring you will find narcissus, auriculas and blue grape hyacinths in drifts between the low-spreading mats of purple-leaved sage. At the beginning of May tall lilacs fitted in between the Irish yew come into flower. The single dark reddish purple variety is *Syringa* 'Souvenir de Louis Spaeth'. 'Capitaine Baltet' is a single pale lilac and the graceful single white variety is 'Vestale'. The long racemes of the standard wisterias planted either side of the seat at the end of the path are flowering by the end of May with tall alliums and yellow asphodels in the borders, together with mauve and white lupins. At the end of May too, the first roses start to bloom. Look out for the pale pink rugosa 'Fru Dagmar Hastrup' and the famous old 'Fantin-Latour' on the left-hand side, heavily double pale pink blooms with a scent that sends you reeling.

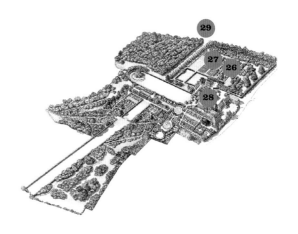

The Rose Walk in May, when lilacs and standard wisterias are among the principal features.

27 THE NEW ORCHARD

During the Second World War Hidcote supplied four hospitals with produce from this vast area, but it is not run as a kitchen garden any longer. When the Trust first took over at Hidcote, shrubs for sale were propagated and grown on here. Now masses of spare plants for the garden are lined out in beds separated by paths and old espalier fruit trees. A new orchard has been planted at the far end. The greenhouse is not open to visitors.

28 THE GARDEN YARD

The tree that dominates the yard, growing against the thatched barn, is a magnificent handkerchief tree, *Davidia involucrata vilmoriniana*. The huge creamy white bracts that give it its common name flutter between the pale green leaves in May. The holly-hedged enclosure with its clipped topiary domes was formerly the drying circle. A superb old wisteria lolls over the corrugated-iron roof of the old loose boxes beyond. At the beginning of May the flowers are still in fish-like bud. The flowers come later in the month. Against the wall of the shop is an unusual false acacia, *Robinia x holdtii*. The blue paint that now is such a feature of Hidcote was the Trust's choice, not Johnston's. 'I should like the entrance gates repainted Snowshill blue instead of the present dowdy yellow-green', wrote Jack Rathbone, the then Secretary of the National Trust (a decision made by the Gardens Committee in May 1961). The colour was later adopted throughout. A cousin of the popular annual sweet pea is used as ground cover under the philadelphus. This pea, *Lathyrus vernus*, is perennial, making useful mounds of foliage studded with small, purple flowers.

29 THE BEECH AVENUE

Through a wrought-iron gate on the north side of the Theatre Lawn is the Beech Avenue running north to one of the distinctive gates at Hidcote copied from that at Cleeve Prior Manor shown in Jekyll and Weaver's *Gardens for Small Country Houses*.

The Beech Avenue.

Echinops ritro 'Globe Thistle' in the Old Garden.

1 THE COURTYARD

Even in the height of summer, strong foliage remains one of the great pleasures of this courtyard: the handsome leaves of *Magnolia delavayi* and gaunt *Mahonia lomariifolia* in the corner to the right, the spiky grey foliage of *Kniphofia caulescens* to the right of the exit from the shop. By June the purple potato flower (*Solanum crispum* 'Glasnevin') has started a display that continues all summer and the huge bush of *Cotoneaster glaucophyllus serotinus* hums with the sound of bees. The smell of mock orange hangs in the air, drowning the fainter scent of the dark violet-purple rambler rose 'Violette' climbing up the gatepost by the far entrance. By July schizophragma is flowering against the wall of the small chapel. It looks very like a climbing hydrangea, but the bracts are spoon-shaped round the central cluster of flowers. Lavender 'Hidcote' and the purple hebe 'Autumn Glory' flower at its feet.

By July too, the special 'Hidcote' hypericum will be in flower behind the grey leaves of the kniphofia and the first flowers will be showing on the hydrangeas and fuchsias. Replacing the rose on the gate pillar is the well-known fuchsia 'Mrs Popple' and a pale pink-flowered version of the wild *Fuchsia magellanica*. In the corner of the courtyard is the pale pink lacecap *Hydrangea macrophylla* 'Lilacina' and to the left of the blue door the elegant white 'Veitchii'.

Campanula latiloba and *Astrantia major* in the Old Garden with *Rosa* 'Goldfinch' over the archway.

2 THE OLD GARDEN

Old mushroom-like staddle-stones (traditionally used to support hay ricks) make the path here, the rhomboid shapes of the bases contrasting with the rounds of the tops. The colour scheme in the two main borders centres round soft blues and pinks. Tall clumps of *Iris monspur* 'Cambridge Blue' provide good foliage as well as thin fleur-de-lis flowers, pale blue with yellow throats. The borders are not matched, though some plants – the iris, *Rosa glauca* – are repeated on both sides. Anchusa, brilliant magenta mounds of *Geranium psilostemon*, campanulas (*C. latiloba* 'Hidcote Amethyst', *C. lactiflora* 'Loddon Anna', *C. latifolia*), astrantia and the purple-smudged flowers of *Philadelphus* 'Belle Etoile' dominate the June border, with, towards the end of the month, big bushes of hybrid musk roses such as the rich pink 'Felicia'.

By July the low-growing pink floribunda rose 'Nathalie Nypels' raised in Holland in 1919 starts a display which continues the whole of the summer. Tender plants, such as salvias, argyranthemums, felicias and osteospermums, settle into the gaps left by the earlier-flowering tulips. In the border along the wall on the north side, tall wands of azure blue *Salvia uliginosa*, coaxed on in the greenhouse, are already leaning over phlox (*P. paniculata* 'Alba'). The oak tubs along the side border on the right-hand side are once again planted with tender pomegranates as they were in Johnston's time. There are sprawling mounds of the herbaceous clematis, *C. integrifolia* 'Hendersonii', with nodding blue flowers standing on long stems above the foliage. Under the cedar is pink oxalis.

The centre borders are dominated by exotic-looking tall pink salvias (*S. involucrata* 'Bethellii' and 'Boutin'), until at the end of July the dahlias begin to flower. These are a great feature of the Old Garden in the second half of summer and bloom until the first frosts stop them in their tracks. The very tall dark purple one is 'Admiral Rawlings', the pale one with mauve staining the edges of the petals is 'Eveline', the pink 'Gerrie Hoek'. The semi-tender argyranthemums take a little while to get into their stride too, but in July the pink powder-puff flowers of 'Mary Wootton' are mingling with the pale blue heads of *Viola cornuta*. The pale yellow *Osteospermum* 'Buttermilk' provides a gentle contrast with clumps of pale apricot day lilies. In the foreground, near the entrance from the Circle, a superb grass, *Pennisetum orientale*, comes into flower, with feathery grey-pink heads like the hairiest kind of caterpillar. Blue-flowered felicias are also best suited to the front of a border. In the Old Garden their bright blue daisy flowers contrast well with the pink 'Nathalie Nypels' rose.

By the end of July tall spikes of eremurus (Fox-Tail Lily) fill the narrow side border where they contrast with the brilliant blue-hooded flowers of *Salvia patens*. The tender *Isoplexis canariensis* with its orange candelabras complement the magnificent displays of lilies and cestrums. The sprawling plant of the white *Clematis viticella* 'Alba Luxurians' used as ground cover.

In the double borders *Yucca flaccida* comes into flower. This is a particularly graceful species, with narrow, greyish leaves, drooping at the tips. Tall spikes of brilliant blue salvias contrast well with white cactus dahlias. The dwarf mauve *Aster x thompsonii* 'Nana' and mounds of pink argyranthemum come into their own in August, though nothing can compete with the exuberance of the dahlias cleverly buttressed and staked against the weather. White cactus dahlias ('My Love') jostle clumps of *Aster x frikartii*, the best of the Michaelmas daisies with big shaggy flowers of mauve, yellow-centred. You can't adjust the volume on dahlias, though. They sing *fortissimo* or not at all.

The narrow borders underneath the cottage at the far right-hand edge of the Old Garden run by way of a gravel and stone path to the back of the Maple Garden. The border under the wall was specially made up with lime-free soil to grow rhododendrons and other calcifuge shrubs. By June the blue Himalayan poppies (*Meconopsis x sheldonii*) are just finishing, but there are enchanting dactylorhiza, small orchid-like roscoeas and *Allium sphaerocephalon*. Later in the summer you may see white agapanthus and the handsome foliage of *Francoa sonchifolia*. Fluffy purple heads appear on top of the tall dark stems of *Eupatorium purpureum*, together with greenish-white spires from *Veratrum album*.

Argyranthemum 'Snow Storm', campanula and *Eremurus robustus* (foxtail lilies) in the Old Garden.

Tour of the Garden

Rosa 'Cornelia' (left) by the gateway to the Old Garden in summer.

Deutzia 'Magician' (opposite), *Rosa* 'Felicia' and lupins in the Old Garden with the yew hedge bordering the White Garden to the left.

3 THE WHITE GARDEN

A path of small, formal square paving-stones leads from the Old Garden into the White Garden with its stylised topiary birds. They are not all the same. On the right-hand side the birds have tails at right angles to their bodies. On the left, the tails curl over like squirrels. There are curves everywhere here: on the tops of the topiary arches over the hedge openings, in the balusters of box leading to the cedar lawn and the drums on which the birds sit. The hedges are dripping with the flame red flower, *Tropaeolum speciosum*. The yew cone takes the gardeners a whole day to put up the scaffolding round this feature and another eight man-hours to clip.

In June the great mounds of crambe are just coming into flower like huge cow parsleys. There are white Canterbury bells and a very pale floribunda rose 'Gruss an Aachen', creamy white flowers overlaid with soft pink. It was raised in Germany, just two years after Johnston came to Hidcote, and flowers throughout the summer. *Lamium maculatum* 'White Nancy' and *Artemisia arborescens* x 'Powis Castle' are used as ground cover.

Later there are white phlox, *Anaphalis triplinervis* and osteospermums with tall sweetly scented white nicotianas and the pale variegated leaves of *Fuchsia magellanica molinae*.

Lilacs in bloom in the Circle (right)

Phlox, acanthus and artemisia in the White Garden (June).

THE MAPLE GARDEN

The vista through from the Maple Garden to the far end of the Old Garden is accentuated by the use of the same Regency-style iron seats at either end. The maple by the seat, a type of *Acer palmatum dissectum* Atropurpureum, is superb. And the shape of this garden is pleasing with its two raised beds either side, the shapes curving like the apse of a church. The spring hyacinths in the centre beds have been replaced by formal blocks of *Heliotrope* 'Lord Robert', with lines of silver artemisia down the centre. Vivid mounds of magenta-flowered *Geranium psilostemon* dominate the raised beds either side. The pale hydrangea with heads starting pale green, turning to cream is *H. arborescens discolor* 'Sterilis'. The architectural cardoons stand proudly above the surrounding plants. In June look out for the rambling rose 'Paul's Himalayan Musk' tumbling out of the yew tree on the left-hand side of the path by the stream.

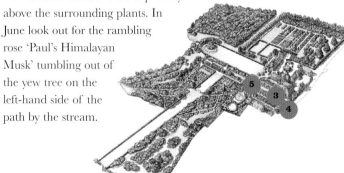

THE CIRCLE

After its explosion of lilac blossom in spring, the Circle quietens and the soft dusky blue of the *Ceanothus x delileanus* 'Gloire de Versailles' and a few Welsh poppies (*Meconopsis cambrica*) drift on into summer edged with *Lavandula* 'Munstead'. In design terms the Circle is vital. It acts as a pivot between two arms of the garden. As one looks west from the Circle, the view stretches between the dramatic Red Borders, through the hornbeam stilts and out through the gates at the end of the garden. Looking south, a much narrower vista carries you through the Fuchsia Garden, over the Bathing Pool and into the corresponding green circle at the extreme edge of the garden. The grass circle with its brick paving is certainly circular, but the boundaries are not. We just assume that they must be, camouflaged as they are by the tall growth of the lilacs. The boundaries are borrowed from other areas: wide-leaved holly mixed with copper beech are woven together to form a tapestry effect which typifies the Arts and Crafts style. This introduces the colour theme to come with yew on the side that abuts the Theatre Lawn and fancy ironwork at the entrance to the Old Garden. The plain grass circle in the centre has to work hard to overcome the disparate elements and uneven parameters of the boundary.

6 THE RED BORDERS

These borders get dressed for summer at the beginning of June, when huge wheelbarrow loads of cannas and lobelias and other exotica are brought down from their shelters in the Kitchen Garden and planted out amongst the permanent inhabitants of the border: purple-leaved nut and maple, purple-leaved cherries, including *Prunus cerasifera* 'Pissardii' and the surprising *Pinus mugo*. The cordylines are plunged in their pots but the cannas, dahlias, verbenas and lobelias are bedded out. When they are lifted in the autumn, the clumps of cannas and lobelias are split up. They are replanted in eight and five-inch pots and overwintered under glass.

With the poppies and the tulips finished, dark foliage dominates the border, with mounds of purple sage, carpets of dark bugle and regular clumps of *Heuchera micrantha*, its dark green leaves flushed with bronze. By the end of the month the well-known floribunda rose 'Frensham' is adding splashes of pure red, and huge panther lilies (*L. pardalinum*), up to seven feet high, crane over bronze explosions of cordyline. A haze of buff flower surrounds the heavy bulk of purple-leaved cotinus. Dark blue delphiniums slotted in along the back of the border make the contrasting reds seem even redder.

These borders are at their most sumptuous by late July. Then, all the tender plants bedded out at the start of June are beginning to flower and the bold clumps of double orange day lilies (*Hemerocallis fulva* 'Kwanso Flore Pleno') used at intervals in the foreground of both borders are in full flow. The lobelias, used much more in Edwardian gardens than they are in modern ones, are stunning. The green-leaved variety is 'Cherry Ripe'. The others, 'Bees Flame' and 'Will Scarlet', have purple leaves. Red dahlias have begun their display too, but they come on strongest when the lobelias start to fade.

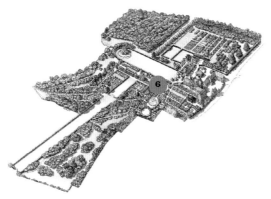

Delphinium 'Startling', *Lilium pardalinum* and *Salvia fulgens* in the Red Borders.

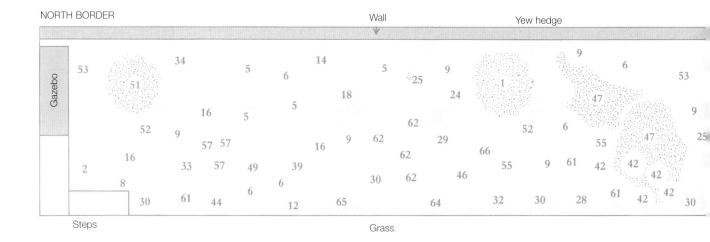

1 *Acer platanoides* 'Crimson King'
2 *Aconitum* 'Spark's Variety'
3 *Ajuga reptans* 'Atropurpurea'
4 *Begonia* 'Hatton Castle'
5 *Buddleja* 'Black Knight'
6 *Canna indica* 'Le Roi Humbert'
7 *Cimicifuga racemosa*
8 *Clematis viticella* 'Kermesina'
9 *Cordyline australis purpurea*
10 *Cordyline australis purpurea* (narrow leaf form)
11 *Corylus maxima* 'Purpurea'
12 *Cosmos atrosanguineus*
13 *Cotinus atropurpureus*
14 *Crocosmia* 'Lucifer'
15 *Dahlia* 'Alva's Doris'
16 *D.* 'Bishop of Llandaff'
17 *D.* 'Bloodstone'

18 *D.* 'Doris Day'
19 *D.* 'Grenadier'
20 *D.* 'Kochelsee'
21 *D.* 'Red Diamond'
22 *D.* 'Red Pygmy'
23 *D.* 'Yvonne'
24 *Delphinium* 'Startling'
25 *Fuchsia fulgens*
26 *F.* 'Rufus'
27 *Geum* 'Borisii'
28 *Hebe* 'Amy'
29 *Hemerocallis* 'Alan'
30 *H. fulva* 'Kwanso Flore Pleno'
31 *H.* 'Stafford'
32 *Heuchera* 'Palace Purple'
33 *Kniphofia uvaria*
34 *Lilium pardalinum*
35 *Lobelia cardinalis* 'Bees Flame'

36 *L. card.* 'Cherry Ripe'
37 *L. card.* 'Queen Victoria'
38 *L. card.* 'Will Scarlet'
39 *Miscanthus sinensis* 'Gracillimus'
40 *Papaver* 'Beauty of Livermere'
41 *P.* 'May Queen'
42 *Pelargonium* 'Generale Championette'
43 *P.* 'Hanry Jacoby'
44 *Penstemon* 'Schoenholzeri'
45 *Phlox* 'Prince of Orange'
46 *Phormium tenax*
47 *Pinus mugo* with *Clematis* 'Viticella Rubra'
48 *Polygonum amplexicaule*
49 *Potentilla* 'Gibson's Scarlet'
50 *Prunus cerasifera* 'Pissardii'
51 *P. spinosa* 'Purpurea'
52 *Pulmonaria saccharata*

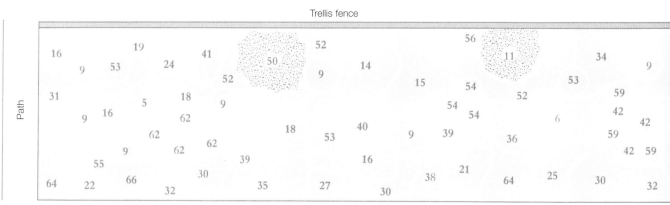

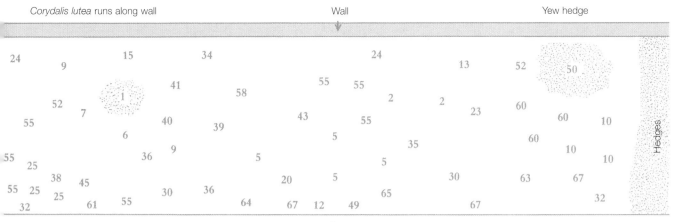

Corydalis lutea runs along wall   Wall   Yew hedge

Grass

53 *Rheum palmatum* 'Atrosanguineum'

54 *Rosa* 'Evelyn Fison'

55 *R.* 'Frensham'

56 *R.* 'Josephine Bruce, Climbing'

57 *R.* 'Marlena'

58 *R. moyesii* 'Geranium'

59 *R.* 'Orange Triumph'

60 *R.* 'Super Star'

61 *Salvia elegans*

62 *S. fulgens*

63 *S. microphylla neurepia*

64 *S. officinalis atropurpurea*

65 *Verbena* 'Huntsman'

66 *V.* 'Lawrence Johnston'

67 *Viola labradorica*

Trellis fence

Grass   Steps

'Bishop of Llandaff' dahlia pays rent twice in this border, for its handsome bronze foliage has its own beauty long before the brilliant single red flowers begin to appear. 'Grenadier' has foliage that is almost as good, setting off its double red flowers. Other dahlias used here are 'Bloodstone', the medium decorative variety 'Red Diamond' and the small cactus varieties 'Alva's Doris' and 'Doris Day'.

Tender fuchsias and salvias need time to build up to their best performance too, so wait until late July or August to see rich *Salvia fulgens*, the Cardinal Sage introduced from Mexico at the beginning of the nineteenth century. It grows to about three feet with lush foliage and lippy flowers of traffic light red. Its cousin, *S. microphylla neurepia*, came from Mexico at the same time but is bigger, with equally vivid flowers. The fuchsias are mostly types of *F. fulgens*, such as 'Rufus', with lush, dark foliage and long, thin tubular flowers, orange-red rather than purplish.

The most lustrous effect comes from the cannas, especially when sunlight shines through their huge paddle-shaped leaves. Only faithful brigades in Parks Departments all over the country kept these magnificently tropical-looking plants from disappearing altogether, after they had fallen out of favour in private gardens. The variety used at Hidcote is 'Le Roi Humbert'. They have tubers like a dahlia's and are equally irresistible to slugs when the new foliage first unfurls from the base. The flowers are like flames.

The Red Borders looking towards the Gazebos and the Stilt Garden (below), and towards the Old Garden and the Cedar of Lebanon (right).

7 THE STILT GARDEN

It is believed that this area was planted not only to lead the eye on to the Vale of Evesham, but was also used to entertain Johnston's guests with a game of boules. The Stilt Garden, a very French idea, and the Gazebos were added in the second phase of the development of Hidcote. There would have been a lot of earth moving to do here, for the ground rises steeply from the Red Borders. Turning to look through the Gazebo doors along the Long Walk, you realise how steeply the land falls away here too. The beds at the end are edged with yew rather than box, with fountains of pampas foliage and the bloodless flowers of Vatican sage, *Salvia sclarea turkestanica*. In each bed is a paulownia, pruned heavily at regular intervals to stimulate a supply of large fresh leaves. The equally large leaves of the vine *Vitis coignetiae* sprawl over the margins of the right-hand bed. Anchusas ('Loddon Royalist') dominate the beds in June with the yellow spires of self-sown verbascum. In August the gardeners begin the exacting task of trimming the hornbeam hedges in the Stilt Garden. It is all done by eye. Scaffolding, built like a siege tower, gives them at least a firm footing.

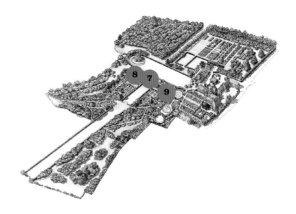

8 THE ALPINE TERRACE

At the end, by the pavilions, a magnificent *Cytisus battandieri* with spiky grey foliage fills the air in June with its pineapple scent. It is believed that Johnston brought this plant back from a trip to Morocco. Hummocks of *Aethionema grandiflorum*, tall spikes of the *Gladiolus byzantinus* and the fleshly foliaged succulent *Drosanthemum hispidum* furnish the south-facing terraces throughout the summer months. The yellow daisy-like flowers of the *Euryops pectinatus* soak up the warm sunshine.

9 THE WINTER BORDER

The background to this is the square-patterned wooden trellis that divides it from the Red Borders behind, and it occasionally borrows stray visitors from this border for its own. Thalictrum thrives under the big magnolia and by August there are sheets of *Strobilanthes atropurpureus*. This is a plant better seen in the morning than the afternoon, for the flowers, a gorgeous blue when they first come out, fade to a less attractive purple as they age. Opposite the Winter Border is the recently replanted Fern Dell containing Jurassic-like tree ferns, ferns and rockii hybrid tree peonies from China. Opposite too is an inviting cool bower of limes. A mosaic of shadows patterns the ground when the sun shines through it.

The Stilt Garden looking west through Heaven's Gate.

10 MRS WINTHROP'S GARDEN

Blue and yellow flowers continue the theme that was started in spring with golden creeping Jenny and blue violas. The creeping Jenny (*Lysimachia nummularia* 'Aurea') continues to spread over the low central beds, eventually dripping over the edges like custard over a tart. In June yellow alliums (*A. moly*) poke out of the carpet. By late July dwarf blue *Agapanthus* 'Lilliput' have replaced them. A froth of alchemilla lines the paths at the top end of the garden until it is sheared down in August. The same greeny-yellow flowers appear on tall stands of *Thalictrum speciosissimum*, which has finely cut leaves of steely blue-green. There are tall euphorbias, yellow Turk's cap lilies and brilliant blue *Salvia patens* in June. On the brick plinths stand pots of bronze cordyline and variegated agaves.

Mounds of *Hypericum* 'Hidcote' light up the ground underneath the rustling Trachycarpus palms. Tall dark blue monkshoods (*Aconitum napellus*) stand in blocks either side of the exit to the Stream Garden. By July the exuberant golden hops in the corners have left their tripods and are clambering over the copper beech hedge.

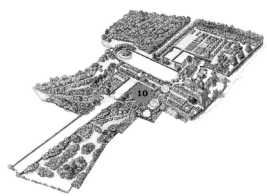

Mrs Winthrop's Garden with its blue and yellow planting, including *Alchemilla mollis* and bronze cordylines in ornamental pots.

Mrs Winthrop's Garden with its sundial looking towards the beech hedge separating this garden from the Winter Border.

Mrs Winthrop's Garden with the sundial upon the pillar from the second Kew Bridge 1789-1899.

Tour of the Garden

11 THE FUCHSIA GARDEN

Because the central design is kept so low – a parterre of box-edged beds filled with dwarf fuchsias – you are perhaps more conscious here than anywhere else of the beauty of Hidcote's hedges: intricate tapestries of copper beech, hollies, box and yew. Between the Fuchsia Garden and the Bathing Pool Garden is a box hedge, about four feet high with yew birds facing each other over the steps down to the pool.

The variegated fuchsia, *F. magellanica* 'Variegata', makes a good foliage feature in the central oval before it ever comes into flower. The bushy dwarf fuchsia 'Tom Thumb', raised in France in the 1850s, is used in the right-hand triangular beds, the paler 'Lady Thumb' in the left-hand beds. The pea-like flower of the *Indigofera heterantha* contrasts well with the red-brick walls. In the corner is the unusual-looking evergreen *Pittosporum dallii*.

Fuchsia magellanica 'Variegata'.

12 THE BATHING POOL GARDEN

'Iceberg' roses grow either side of the steps down to this garden with a spreading *Magnolia x soulangeana* on the left-hand side, underplanted with a quiet, elegant colony of shuttlecock ferns. The unusual *Corydalis ochroleuca* with white flowers and filigree foliage hang out of the retaining wall at the back. In front is a narrow curving border, home first to the beautiful Himalayan poppy, then wands of blue-flowered gentian, *G. asclepiadea*, followed in late August by the magnificent spires of white bottle brush flowers on *Cimicifuga racemosa*. At the far end, steps rise to the third circle in the line from the one beyond the Fuchsia Garden. The steps are actually made from reclaimed clay roof tiles laid on end. Looking back that way, you see tiers of hedges rising parallel to one another, the low hedge of box in the Fuchsia Garden surmounted by the mixed hedge of beech and holly behind, with the yew hedge of the Theatre Lawn on top of that.

The small courtyard that leads off the Bathing Pool Garden is paved in red tiles that look too much like a kitchen floor to be entirely successful. Johnston did not spend money on the construction of his paths, paving and walls. Materials were mostly reused from other parts of the house and garden, and the steps and walls were built without proper foundations. But this is a pleasant, contemplative place to sit on hot days. Big *Hosta sieboldiana* grow in terracotta pots here, together with a matching pair of stag's horn sumachs (*Rhus typhina*), which have to be replaced at regular intervals when they have grown too leggy. Pink bleeding heart and splendid ferns enjoy cool billets at the feet of the walls.

The Bathing Pool Garden.

13 THE POPPY GARDEN

Not so much poppies as hostas, which have spread to make an almost unbroken carpet under hydrangeas, which are at their best from late July. Then both the hostas and the magnificent *Hydrangea aspera* Villosa are in flower. Swags of the huge-leaved *Vitis coignetiae* sprawl over the arch from the courtyard.

14, 16, 19 THE STREAM GARDEN

This is a large and rambling area, made up from four geographically distinct locations. First, there is the area immediately outside the plain green circle into which the path from the Poppy Garden leads. The upper path here takes you to the bog garden and then to the Wilderness, but if you take the first narrow path to the right, it leads past a huge evergreen *Osmanthus forrestii*, with cool slabs of rock underneath, lacy fronds of maidenhair fern (*Adiantum venustum*) and moss, as cool and elegant a combination as you would find in any Japanese garden. This path hugs the boundary of the Bathing Pool Garden to bring you over the stream to a rather indeterminate area east of Mrs Winthrop's Garden. In late August *Kirengeshoma palmata* with shiny black stems and shuttlecock flowers of palest lemon yellow thrives in a corner by the path from the Bathing Pool Garden. In its season, it is the most beautiful thing in the Stream Garden.

Immediately below Mrs Winthrop's Garden is a different part of the Stream Garden. At the top is a newly planted area with *Polygonum* 'Superbum', yellow-flowered *Crocosmia* 'Solfaterre', francoa, perovskia and white lacecap hydrangeas. From here the ground slopes steeply down to the stream which is bordered with huge blocks of hosta and several kinds of ligularia, all of which enjoy the damp conditions here. *L. przewalskii* has black stems, jagged leaves and spires of yellow flowers. Juicy spikes of terracotta flowers, the texture of plush, rise from clumps of rodgersia. They are particularly good contrasted with the rounded blue leaves of hosta and the rich dark blue flowers of tradescantia.

By July plumes of astilbe flowers in pink and deep red rise between the bulky foliage of the skunk cabbage and brunnera. A tall wild-looking phlox, the original *P. paniculata*, billows in a stately fashion in front of the huge mauve panicles on *Hydrangea sargentiana*, and white lacecap hydrangeas. On the far side of the Long Walk is another extensive area of the Stream Garden with a path wandering along the left-hand bank of the little stream to a bridge and an open glade beyond. *Ligularia dentata* 'Desdemona' has rounded dark, almost purple leaves with flaming orange flowers. The largest Indian horse chestnut (*Aesculus indica*) in Britain grows by the bridge. It has candelabra flowers of pink in June. Another path loops back over the higher ground bordering the Long Walk. Ligularias shine out here in June, with ferns erupting amongst them. Pale acid yellow flag irises rise from the stream bed, contrasting with martagon lilies and the last of the magenta primulas. Epimediums, white woodruff and *Ranunculus aconitifolius* 'Flore Pleno', a double white buttercup, are used as ground cover under shrubs on the left-hand side. Since the ilex in this area have been cut back heavily, the plants underneath have grown much better. Veratrums flourish, sending up tall white flower spikes in early July.

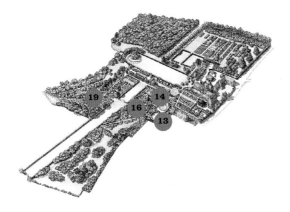

Ranunculus aconitifolius 'Flore Pleno' and Astrantia under *Magnolia campbelli* in the Lower Stream Garden.

17 THE WILDERNESS

Roses are the surprise in the Wilderness in early summer: 'La Mortola' with greyish foliage and creamy white flowers climbing through the holly, and the multiflora rambler 'Francis E. Lester', with large trusses of single flowers, white flushed with pink, tackling a pine. There are plenty more.

The entrance to the Wilderness is planted with bold, large-leaved herbaceous plants: cimicifuga, hostas, ligularia. By the beginning of August hydrangeas are the most mouth-watering things here, especially the lanky, loose-limbed *Hydrangea sargentiana*, with large flat heads of mauve sterile bracts surrounding a central boss of tightly packed bobble flowers. There is a surprising view from the far side of the primula pool towards Mrs Winthrop's Garden, nearer than you thought it could be.

18 THE LONG WALK

'Was it fortuitous that all the long, formal views, ending in an open invitation to explore further, were arranged on ground rising before one?' wrote Graham Stuart Thomas in the 1979 edition of *Gardens of the National Trust*. 'The irresistible urge is in everyone to mount each slope…: a journey ever upwards with the reward at the top.' Manipulating Hidcote's site, which slopes in several directions, was a major challenge to the ingenuity of its owner. The smooth lines of the hornbeam hedge become like stage flats, with us, the garden visitors, as the actors, making our entrances and exits across the wide stage of grass, from the Wilderness to the Stream Garden, from the Stream Garden to the Pillar Garden.

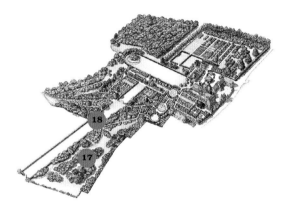

A view through the south Gazebo looking south along another of the main axes of Hidcote, the Long Walk.

20 THE BULB SLOPE

This is very pretty still at the beginning of summer with stands of wild-looking campanulas, white and blue. The campanulas carry this area right through until the middle of July, together with fine clumps of martagon lilies. After this, its season is over.

21 THE ROCK BANK

The bank has been planted with plants that thrive in hot, dry situations. *Cistus x corbariensis* and the pale yellow helianthemum 'Wisley Primrose' cover the bank on the side nearest the Pillar Garden. Khakicoloured whipcord hebes grow further down under the low, spreading limbs of a pine, *P. densiflora* 'Umbraculifera'. At the Stilt Garden end of the Rock Bank is a splendid multi-stemmed ilex. How did it get like this? Were a handful of seedling ilexes all planted together here? Or is this a single tree, sat upon in extreme youth by an overweight spaniel?

By the end of July a brilliant blue bed of *Gentiana septemfida* springs up on the far side of the Rock Bank and the tall walking sticks of the aralia come into bloom, flat creamy heads like elderflower. A creeping slate-blue mallow accompanies an equally low-growing evening primrose (*Oenothera missouriensis*) on its journey to the feet of a broom, whose seedpods explode in the summer sun. The bottom end of the bank has been replanted with a collection of typical scree plants including roscoea, cyclamen and ceratostigma.

22 THE PILLAR GARDEN

The yew pillars dominate this area, poised as if for some stately court dance, advancing towards each other across the central grass lawn, then retreating to their solid square bases to pose until the next visitor has disappeared. It is laid out in a series of parallel paths and beds with mock orange scenting the air in June. These are planted at the top, next to the boundary hedge, *Philadelphus* 'Belle Etoile' with smudgy mauve centres in its abundant creamy white flowers, 'Beauclerk' with a less pronounced mauve stain. When the philadelphus has finished, the huge stands of *Romneya coulteri* come into flower, white tissue paper poppy heads springing from handsome grey foliage. Hedges of lavender line the narrow path and release a different, more pungent fragrance as you brush by them. The peonies, so stunning in May, have completely finished, but you may still catch the faded drumstick heads of the alliums that grow behind them.

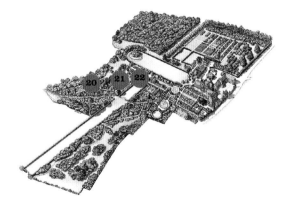

Lilium umbellatum 'Orange Triumph' in the Pillar Garden.

22 THE PILLAR GARDEN continued

On the lower level agapanthus are the stars by late July and continue to look stunning for most of August. Behind them are fuchsias (*F.* 'Margaret', 'Baby Blue Eyes', 'Thompsonii' and 'Kwintet') and, springing between the yew pillars, *Lavandula x intermedia* 'Hidcote Giant' (possibly planted by Johnston himself). The bottom right-hand corner of this garden flames with brilliant orange *Alstroemeria aurantiaca*, a native of southern Chile, set against the equally brilliant yellow of a broom, *Spartium junceum*. More fuel is added to the fire with blazing 'Harlequin' hybrid lilies.

The two big beds below the Pillar Garden have recently been replanted to the original design, as so eloquently described in *Country Life* in 1930. A riot of colour once again greets the eye with an exciting mixture of lilies, roses and clematis.

23 THE THEATRE LAWN

Johnston designed the architectural theatre lawn for spiritual and quiet contemplation. The yew hedges round the lawn are grand and formal, but the hedge that stretches down from the restaurant beside the path has been patched at the bottom with box, which gives quite a different texture..

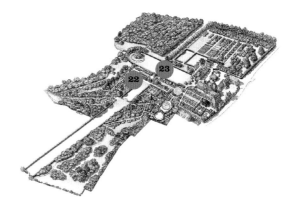

Allium giganteum in the Pillar Garden (top).

Romneya coulteri in the Pillar Garden (left).

Alstroemeria aurantiaca in the Pillar Garden looking towards the hornbeams of the Stilt Garden (right).

24 THE PINE GARDEN AND LILY POOL

Like the Rock Bank, this has a distinctly Mediterranean feeling, with the clipped mophead sweet bays, the pool and the pots of spiky agaves. The raised bed is surrounded by pale potentillas and rock roses, with silver-leaved bright yellow gazanias planted out between them. By August the far side of the pool is fringed with agapanthus, and the pale yellow *Argyranthemum* 'Jamaica Primrose' is smothered with daisy flowers.

The pool itself is surrounded by huge stone troughs with thrifts and sempervivums. The planting round the pool is cool: grey and pale sulphur yellow, coming mostly from cotton lavender, with sea lavender, *Limonium latifolium*, adding clouds of mauve flowers for weeks in late summer. Clipped sweet bays guard the entrance to the small grass court behind this garden. In August pink crinums cluster round the feet of the laurels. The eye-catching variegated bush on the right-hand side of the path that leads to the rose borders is *Euonymus fortunei* 'Silver Queen'.

25 THE PLANT HOUSE

During the summer months the glass fronts are removed to give a pergola effect. The angels trumpets are in full flower with their large hanging yellow flowers. The air is filled with the sweet smell of flowering citrus which will, over the winter, develop into juicy oranges and lemons.

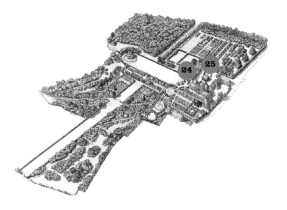

The Lily Pool with lavatera and water lilies.

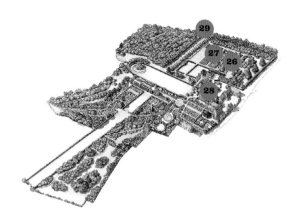

At the entrance to the Rose Walk is a magnificent old robinia, *R. x ambigua* 'Decaisneana', with a bark more furrowed than a bloodhound's forehead. It blossoms in early June with tassels of pink pea-like flowers. The rose garden ahead was Johnston's last innovation at Hidcote, made at the suggestion of his friend Norah Lindsay. Two lines of clipped yew trees mark the centre of the borders and they are planted with old French roses: gallicas, damasks, mosses and their kind. During the 1960s both borders were completely replanted by the Head Gardener, Harry Burrows. Over the next few years, the current garden team will clear a border a year and then fallow it for a year to get rid of the perennial weed.

These borders are usually (one has to be cautious, given the vagaries of the British weather) at their best during the last two weeks in June. Few of these roses are repeat-flowering. 'Vivid', a Bourbon rose raised in this country in 1853, occasionally throws out some extra blooms after its main early summer season. The flowers are very bright magenta pink with a swoony smell. The frilly pink rugosa 'Pink Grootendorst' is more reliable in the matter of repeat-flowering as are the other rugosas in this border, such as 'Fru Dagmar Hastrup'.

The gallicas are well represented, with the very old variety 'Surpasse Tout', deep cerise-maroon, paling as it ages. 'Marcel Bourgouin' was bred in France in 1899, semi-double flowers of rich, deep red. 'Sissinghurst Castle', which was discovered growing in Vita Sackville-West's garden, has a semi-double flower, richly scented, with deep maroon petals, backed by a paler pink. 'Tuscany Superb', raised in this country in 1848, has similar dark red flowers and obligingly few thorns. It does not have the pale reverses of 'Sissinghurst Castle'.

One of the best of the damasks is 'St Nicholas', bred by Johnston's friend Bobbie James and named after his own Hidcote-style garden at Richmond in Yorkshire. It is like a glorified wild dog rose, the same soft pink, but doubled. The foliage is vigorous and downy grey. Unusually for a damask, it is repeat-flowering. 'Mme Zoetmans', bred in France in 1830, has the palest of pink flowers, very double, each with a neat green eye, like the better known damask 'Mme Hardy'. 'La Ville de Bruxelles' has much richer pink flowers than 'Mme Hardy', but with the same heady perfume characteristic of all the damasks.

The moss roses are particularly appealing and one of the best grown here is 'Mousseux du Japon', very heavily mossed on the buds and even on the stalks of the leaves. The flowers are semi-double, a pale lilac pink. 'Lanei', raised in France in 1854, has dark moss surrounding very double deep crimson flowers, which open flat to show a green eye in the centre. 'A Longues Pedoncules' is named for its long flower stalks, heavily encrusted with moss and holding double flowers of soft pink.

When the roses fade, a wide variety of penstemons come into bloom, 'Garnet', 'Hidcote Pink', 'Sour Grapes' and pale blue 'Alice Hindley'. By the first week in August, most of the colour comes from phlox, with pale-coloured deciduous ceanothus catching up fast. The ceanothus are pruned hard back to two buds each April to keep them a manageable size. At the back of the Rose Border, next to the frames and beds of the Kitchen Garden, is a long border with fine late double peonies and the biennial eryngium, *E. giganteum*, known as 'Miss Willmott's ghost'.

27 THE NEW ORCHARD

This was an intensively gardened patch in Johnston's day, where the gardeners grew large amounts of fruit and vegetables, which they sold to local suppliers. Now the area is mostly devoted to raising spare plants for the garden. At the beginning of June, the glasshouse is still full of salvias, geraniums, dahlias, osteospermums, agaves, convolvulus and helichrysum, waiting to move to quarters outside. By July the houses are mostly empty, and the time that has been devoted to looking after them is spent instead on the long summer job of clipping the four and a half miles of hedging in the garden. A hedge of *Rosa mundi* provides a stunning summer display.

Old French roses in the Rose Walk.

28 THE GARDEN YARD

Fuchsias and geraniums replace the earlier-flowering hyacinths and tulips in the tubs. The fuchsia with pale stamens, pink bell and white upswept sepals is 'Hidcote Beauty'. The lead tank is planted with a tender seasonal display that varies each year.

29 THE BEECH AVENUE

During the Summer, the Beech Avenue provides a peaceful, shaded haven where even on the busiest days, few visitors are to be found.

Autumn

Frost is the great dictator of the autumn garden. A few nights of sub-zero temperatures in September can bring an early and precipitate end to the stunning performance of the dahlias in the Old Garden and the Red Borders. The team of gardeners start to put the garden's summer clothes – agaves, cordylines, cannas, lobelias and salvias – away in the greenhouse ready for another season. The Wilderness, the large area of trees and shrubs that lies hidden behind the tall hornbeam hedge of the Long Walk, comes into its own with now-or-never displays from the Japanese maples.

1 THE COURTYARD

The huge bush of *Cotoneaster glaucophyllus serotinus* that hummed with bees in summer is, by September, covered with small dusty claret-coloured berries. On the right-hand side of the exit from the shop, fatsia spreads its glossy leaves, topped in October with creamy drumstick heads of flower. The solanum in the corner to the right of the blue door is still in bloom, with purple potato flowers. Pink nerines sprout in the narrow border beside the chapel. Lemon-coloured poker flowers with pale buff and apricot tips emerge from the grey whorls of foliage of *Kniphofia caulescens*.

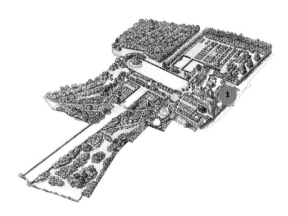

A late autumn frost. Looking along one of the main axes from the Old Garden through the Circle to the Gazebos, the Stilt Garden and Heaven's Gate.

2 THE OLD GARDEN

Provided there are no frosts, autumn continues in an unbroken thread from late summer in the Old Garden. Dahlias are still the most dominant element: the tallest is 'Admiral Rawlings'. There are mounds of the superlative Michaelmas daisy, *Aster x frikartii*, and, in the side border, floppy spires of sky blue flowers from *Salvia uliginosa* and shorter spikes from *S. cacaliifolia*, which has bright green wedge-shaped leaves. The unusual phototropic *S. leucantha* will also be coming back into flower during October. Cyclamen, first pink shuttlecock flowers, then marbled foliage, fill the dry unpromising bed under the cedar tree. Long bristly red hips hang from the Chinese rose, *R. setipoda*, in the border under the wooden arch.

3 THE WHITE GARDEN

The white roses 'Gruss an Aachen' give a generous late display, which often continues until October. Though the acanthus spikes begin to fade, the foliage makes huge glossy mounds, an excellent contrast for white flowers around it. White osteospermums are almost at their best.

4 THE MAPLE GARDEN

By October the foliage of the drooping maple has turned to a soft bracken colour, though the variegated fuchsias, *F. magellanica* 'Versicolor', continue triumphantly to overflow from the east-facing border. Frost may fell the heliotrope in the central beds but *Knautia macedonica* continues to send up branched stems of crimson-purple pincushion flowers.

5 THE CIRCLE

As the leaves change colour in autumn, the hedges round the Circle change too, the copper beech softening to a foxy brown that stays almost until the new buds of spring. The tapestry hedges, mixtures of yew and box, holly and beech, are one of the great glories of Hidcote. Compare these with what Leyland cypress, the modern hedging favourite, has to offer: no changing colour, no texture, nothing except a galloping propensity to block out the light.

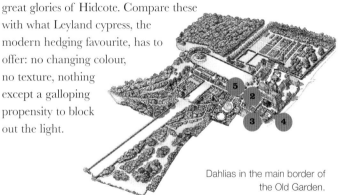

Dahlias in the main border of the Old Garden.

6 THE RED BORDERS

As in the Old Garden, dahlias dominate the borders, glowing against the dark embers of the purple-leaved trees behind. Some of the dahlias, such as 'Bishop of Llandaff' with single red flowers and 'Grenadier' with double, have dark foliage too. In September the tender fuchsias are at their best with lustrous bronzed foliage and long drooping orange-red tube flowers. Some of the roses, such as *R. moyesii*, bear excellent hips, and the brilliant red verbena 'Lawrence Johnston', which grew wild in his French garden at La Serre de la Madone, matches them in the intensity of its colour. Strong upright sheaves of the ornamental grass, *Miscanthus sinensis* 'Gracillimus', by now five feet high, contrast with the symmetrical stiff fountains of cordyline.

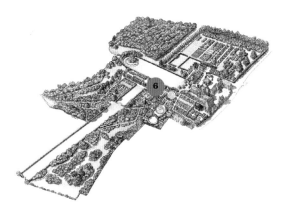

Dahlia 'Grenadier' in the Red Borders (top).

Dahlia 'Doris Day' in the Red Borders (left).

Rosa 'Frensham' in the Red Borders looking towards one of the Gazebos and the Stilt Garden beyond (opposite).

Tour of the Garden

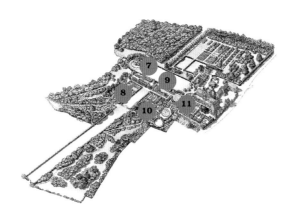

7 THE STILT GARDEN

In Johnston's time the pampas grasses *Cortaderia fulvida* were used at regular intervals along the back of the Red Borders. They have been replaced by *Cortaderia selloana* 'Pumila', which is now in full flight here. By October there is a change in colour in the stiff, rough leaves of the vine *Vitis coignetiae* that drapes itself over the low yew hedge of the small enclosures in the Stilt Garden.

8 THE ALPINE TERRACE

Towards the end of October the glass frames will be placed into position to protect the tender plants from the cold and wet. This will take two gardeners two days to complete. In the top terrace beautiful acidantheras can be seen flowering in early autumn. The succulents *Opuntia grandis* and *Aeonium* 'Zwartkop' are also worth a look.

9 THE WINTER BORDER

Hips and berries are one of the great joys of the autumn scene at Hidcote. By October the big vine (*Vitis coignetiae*) draped over the pavilion will be changing colour with its brilliant red and orange autumn foliage. With winter looming the winter jackets for the tree ferns will be stuffed into their tender crowns.

10 MRS WINTHROP'S GARDEN

The extremely narrow entrance through the beech hedge into this garden room makes its discovery all the more pleasurable. The dark blue hooded flowers of the monkshoods continue through autumn and the borders of alchemilla in the upper beds refresh themselves with new foliage. Frost can strike early in the Cotswolds and before the end of the season the cordylines and agaves in their pots may have been bundled into the safety of the glasshouse.

11 THE FUCHSIA GARDEN

This is at its best in late summer and early autumn when the fuchsias flower at full tilt. The variegated fuchsia is *F. magellanica* 'Variegata'. The smaller beds have the dwarf hybrids 'Tom Thumb' and 'Lady Thumb'. The hedges at the back and to the right-hand side of this enclosure are particularly intricate with mixes of holly (*Ilex x altaclerensis* 'Hodginsii'), yew, copper beech and box.

A terracotta basket pot containing *Fuchsia* 'Thalia' with *Aconitum* 'Sparks Variety' on the steps up to the Red Borders.

12 THE BATHING POOL GARDEN

The generous 'Iceberg' roses give a second season of flower here in early autumn, holding their own until the magnificent pampas grass erupts into bloom. Tall bottle-brush flowers of cimicifuga are thrown into sharp relief by the dark background of the yew hedge. Already by the beginning of September the leaves of the stag's horn sumach in the courtyard may be beginning to turn. By October only a few tattered flags will be left.

13 THE POPPY GARDEN

Until the inevitable collapse of the hostas, these give a wonderfully lush effect, their foliage underpinning the fading blooms of the hydrangeas. The rough-leaved *Vitis davidii* draped over the entrance from the courtyard gets better and better as the season advances. From the quiet roundel of grass beyond the Poppy Garden you get a beautifully composed view back over the Bathing Pool, past the topiary birds to the mixed hedges beyond.

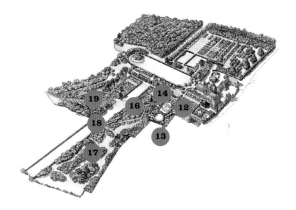

14, 16, 19 THE STREAM GARDEN

There are still new arrivals here: the pale creamy yellow flowers of kirengeshoma borne above the handsome, jagged foliage, the brilliant red flowers of the kaffir lily (*Schizostylis coccinea* 'Major') under the cherry at the entrance to the Lower Stream Garden and the weird spotted purple flowers of the toad lily (*Tricyrtis formosana*). Gentler colour comes from the dying foliage of the big-leaved hostas planted along the stream and from the fading heads of the unusual double-flowered hydrangea, *H. involucrata* 'Hortensis'. The dying fronds of the shuttlecock ferns fan out on the ground like ballet skirts round upright fruiting stems, dark and rough.

17 THE WILDERNESS

Tall yellow senecio, white cimicifuga and blue monkshood still bloom in September in the border of large-leaved perennials that you pass coming into The Wilderness from the Long Walk. If you approach directly from the small grass roundel, the wonderful orange and red leaves of a spindle, *Euonymus europaeus*, will be the chief treat. There are ghostly white berries on *Sorbus hupehensis* and waxy yellow clusters on *Viburnum opulus* 'Xanthocarpum'. Bunches of purplish red keys hang from some of the maples, which predominate in this section. You have to wait until October for the full roar of their autumn performance. The berries on the big holly (*Ilex x altaclerensis* 'Camelliifolia') are fully ripe by the end of September and glow brilliantly against the glossy evergreen foliage. As you emerge at the top end of The Wilderness, where it gives on to farmland, a sheet of colchicums provides a final surprise.

18 THE LONG WALK

All through late summer and autumn the team of Hidcote gardeners will be engaged in trimming the daunting expanse of the hornbeam hedges. From the high land at the end of the vista, you are in a position to see how cleverly Johnston manipulated the sloping ground of the garden into a series of level, roughly south-facing terraces.

The Long Walk looking towards the Gazebo.

20 THE BULB SLOPE

The maple, *Acer palmatum*, against the boundary begins to colour and waxy berries droop from the sober mounds of berberis. If the wind does not find them first, the leaves of the fine Indian horse chestnut, *Aesculus indica*, at the bottom of the slope by the stream turn a foxy burnt orange.

21 THE ROCK BANK

Berries of extraordinary metallic blue are *Viburnum davidii*'s contribution in autumn. The shrub, introduced from western Sichuan in 1904, is handsome at all seasons, with particularly good evergreen leaves, broad and pointed. The veins, running the length of the leaf, are deeply incised. Blue gentians, *G. septemfida* and *G. sino-ornata* 'Kingfisher', flower vividly at the base of the scree.

22 THE PILLAR GARDEN

Fuchsias hold the stage here during September, particularly the soft mounds of the variegated fuchsia along the top walk. The willing geranium 'Buxton's Variety', blue with a white eye, covers the ground where the summer lilies bloomed. For a curiously tropical view in September, look back from the Long Walk end of the Pillar Garden to the jagged leaves of the aralia on the Rock Bank, silhouetted against the sky, the whole enclosed by a lush, thick backdrop of evergreen ilex trees. By October pink nerines replace the agapanthus in the narrow border by the lawn.

23 THE THEATRE LAWN

By late September a few autumn crocuses will be pushing their noses through the grass under the young beech trees on its dais. The curve of the yew hedge is echoed in the shape of the enclosing yew hedge behind. On the north side a tall avenue of beeches, particularly brilliant in October, leads to curved blue wooden gates and the outside world.

The Pillar Garden viewed from above the Stilt Garden.

24 THE PINE GARDEN AND LILY POOL

The raised circular bed, 'foaming with rock roses of every shade, a lovely surprise, as light as spindrift, shot with many colours the rainbow does not provide', was beautifully brought to life by Vita Sackville-West, writing about Hidcote in 1949. Bright yellow gazanias and potentilla grow there too. By the pool, the generous daisy flowers of *Argyranthemum* 'Jamaica Primrose' contrast beautifully with the stiff formal lines of the agaves in their pots. Tall, swan-necked crinums open their pink trumpet flowers on top of stout, tall stems. Mounds of grey foliage – *Helichrysum microphyllum*, santolina and lavender – soften the straight edges of the lily pool.

25 THE PLANT HOUSE

During October the glass fronts are replaced to provide protection to the tender exotic plants found within the shelter. If you look carefully you will see the small green developing fruit on the citrus plants.

26 THE ROSE WALK

The roses, few of them repeat-flowering, give way to pale blue clouds of ceanothus in September. There are still occasional spikes of flower on the penstemons, though their best season has passed.

27 THE NEW ORCHAR

The orchard behind the Rose Walk is planted with an interesting collection of old varieties of apple. On a still day, the air is full of their complex aromas: the smell of harvest festivals, of autumn. As leaves begin to fall, evergreens come into their own. The glasshouses, emptied of their exotic occupants at the beginning of June, now begin to fill up again as frost-tender agaves, cannas and cordylines are brought under cover at the end of their season.

28 THE GARDEN YARD

Purple liriope, a useful late-flowering perennial, starts to flower at the beginning of September in the narrow border behind the handkerchief tree, and Japanese anemones flourish amongst the ferns.

29 THE BEECH AVENUE

Autumn sees the Beech Avenue carpeted with the fallen leaves.

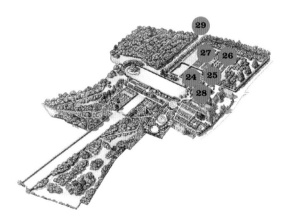

The Lily Pool with its lilies surrounded by gazania and agapanthus.

Further Reading

Mea Allan (1973). *E. A. Bowles and His Garden at Myddelton House 1865–1954*, London, Faber & Faber.

Ethne Clarke (1989). *Hidcote The Making of a Garden*, London, Michael Joseph.

Collingwood Ingram (1970). *A Garden of Memories*, London, H.F. & G. Witherby.

Gertrude Jekyll (1908). *Colour in the Flower Garden*, London, Country Life & George Newnes, Ltd.

Gertrude Jekyll and Lawrence Weaver (1912). *Gardens for Small Country Houses*, London, Country Life.

Gertrude Jekyll (1900). *Home and Garden*, London, Longmans, Green, and Co.

Gertrude Jekyll (1901). *Wood and Garden*, London, Longmans, Green, and Co.

Thomas H. Mawson (1907, 1912). *The Art and Craft of Garden Making*, London, B.T. Batsford, Ltd.

Brenda McLean (1997). *A Pioneering Plantsman A.K. Bulley and the Great Plant Hunters*, London, The Stationery Office.

Brenda McLean (2004). *George Forrest Plant Hunter*, Antique Collectors' Club.

Howard Pease (ed) (1924). *The History of the Northumberland (Hussars) Yeomanry 1819–1919 with supplement to 1923*, London, Constable and Company Ltd.

Karl B. Spurgin (1902). *On Active Service with the Northumberland and Durham Yeomen under Lord Methuen (South Africa 1900–1901)*, London and Newcastle-on-Tyne, Walter Scott Publishing Co. Ltd.

Journal Articles:

Laurence (sic) Johnson (sic) (1929), 'Some Flowering Plants of Kilimanjaro', *The New Flora and Fauna*, No.5, Vol 11, October, 11–6.

Norah Lindsay (1948), 'Hidcote Manor', *House and Garden*, v.3, April, 46–51.

Russell Page (1934), 'Hidcote Manor Microcosm', *The Listener*, 22 August, 321–3.

Graham Pearson and Susan Pearson (2004), 'The Hunt for Hidcote's Horticultural Treasures', *Country Life*, 19 February, 94–97.

Vita Sackville-West (1949), 'Hidcote Manor', *J. Royal Hort. Soc.* 74, No. 11, November, 476–81.

H. Avray Tipping (1930), 'Hidcote Manor, Gloucestershire The Seat of Mr. Lawrence Johnston', *Country Life*, 22 February, 286–94.

H. Avray Tipping (1930), 'Early Summer at Hidcote Manor', *Country Life*, 23 August, 231–3.

Picture Credits

National Trust Books are committed to respecting the intellectual property rights of others. We have therefore taken all reasonable efforts to ensure that the reproduction of all content on these pages is done with the full consent of copyright owners. If you are aware of any unintentional omissions please contact the company directly so that any necessary corrections can be made for future editions.

Courtesy of Gloucestershire Archives/Bruton Knowles & Co, D2299/1021: 15

Courtesy of Gloucestershire Archives/National Trust, D2784/3: 14

Reproduced from the 1885 Ordnance Survey map © Crown Copyright: 16

Reproduced from the London Gazette, Issue No. 27160, 2 February 1900. © Crown Copyright: 11

© Country Life: 26UL, 26LL, 36, 37L, 38U, 38L, 39U, 40U, 41U, 43U

© Derek C. Bull: 13, 18L, 19UR, 20LL, 20LR, 21LL, 24UR, 24 LR, 25LR, 27U, 27L, 28R, 29, 31, 37R, 42U, 42L, 43L, 61, 98, 99

Miles Hadfield: 30

Collingwood Ingram: 33

A. H. Lealand: 19UL, 20UL
Thomas H. Mawson: 19LL

Courtesy of Mickleton Women's Institute: 8

© National Trust, Legal Section: 25UR

© National Trust Archives: 44, 45, 46L, 49, 57

© National Trust/Hidcote: 18U, 19LR, 20UR, 21UR, 21LR, 22LL, 23U, 24UL, 25LL, 26LR, 28LL

©NTPL/Ian Blantern: 9, NTPL/Mark Bolton: 22 U, 81, 97, 102, 113, NTPL/Neil Campbell-Sharp: 134, NTPL/Colin Clarke: 23 L, 127, NTPL/Derek Croucher: 4, 41 L, 75, 76, 86, 90, 91, 92, 103, 106, 111, 112, NTPL/David Dixon: Front Cover, 80, 84, 152, NTPL/Rowan Isaac: 148, NTPL/Andrew Lawson: 2, 40, 64, 139, NTPL/Nick Meers: 6, 51, 114, 136, 144, NTPL/Stephen Robson: 39 L, 70, 72, 77, 78, 94, 95, 96, 104, 118, 119, 121, 122, 124, 126, 134, 140, 142, 145 (both), 147, back cover, NTPL/David Sellman: 88, 100, 108, 110, 123, 129, 133, 135, NTPL/Claire Takacs: 1, 67, 74, 131, 150, NTPL/Mike Williams: 82,

© National Trust Plan of Garden: 68/69,

© National Trust Plan of Red Borders: 116/117

Photo Precision Ltd: 54

Peter Pritchard: 22LR

© Royal Botanical Garden Edinburgh: 35

© Royal Horticultural Society: 46U

© The Times, London, 29 June 1948: 48

The Times, London, 28 June 1948: 47

Courtesy of Mrs. D. M. Williams: 17U, 17L

Index

Page numbers in **bold** denote illustrations